The Illustrated Encyclopedia of Major

Airliners of the World

The Illustrated Encyclopedia of Major

Airliners of the World

David Mondey

CRESCENT BOOKS
New York

Crescent Books

First English edition published by Temple Press
an imprint of Newnes Books 1983

All rights reserved.
This edition published by Crescent Books,
a division of Crown Publishers, Inc.
h g f e d c b a

Printed and bound in Italy

Created and produced by Stan Morse
Aerospace Publishing Ltd
10 Barley Mow Passage
London W4 4PH

© Aerospace Publishing Ltd 1983

Colour profiles and line diagrams © Pilot Press Ltd

All correspondence concerning the content of this volume
should be addressed to Aerospace Publishing Ltd. Trade
enquiries should be addressed to Crescent Books,
New York.

ISBN: 0-517-405032

Library of Congress Catalog Card Number: 83-70 125

PICTURE ACKNOWLEDGEMENTS

The Publishers wish to thank the following people and organizations for their help in supplying photographs for this book.

Jacket front: Alaska Airlines. **Jacket back:** PanAm. **Pages 2/3:** Swissair. **4/5:** UTA. **9.** Austin J. Brown. **10:** British Aerospace. **11:** British Aerospace. **14:** Austin J. Brown. **15:** Ian McFarlane via Editions JP. **16:** Asahi Helicopter. **17:** Airbus Industrie. **24:** Austin J. Brown. **25:** Fotokronikha Tass. **26:** Austin J. Brown. **27:** Austin J. Brown. **28:** Beech. **29:** Pilgrim Airlines. **30:** Beech. **31:** Bristow Helicopter Group. **32:** Bell Helicopter Textron. **33:** Bell Helicopter Textron. **34:** Bell Helicopter Textron. **35:** Avianca. **38:** Air Malta. **39:** Iberia. **40/41:** Trans World Airlines. **42:** Air Europe. British Aerospace. **44:** Flying Tigers. **45:** Wardair Canada. **46/47:** SAS. **48:** Qantas Airways. **49:** Saudia. **51:** British Airways. **53:** American Airlines. **54:** Boeing Vertol Company. **55:** Austin J. Brown. **56:** Philippine Airlines. **59:** British Aerospace. **60:** Philippine Airlines. **61:** British Aerospace. **62:** Prof. Johannes Zopp. **66:** Britten-Norman. **67:** Aurigny. **68:** Britten-Norman. **69:** Flying Tigers. **74:** Austin J. Brown. **75:** Austin J. Brown. **76:** Cessna. **79:** Aspen Airways. **81:** Austin J. Brown. **82:** Austin J. Brown. **83:** F. Pötsch via Editions JP. **84:** Ueli Klee via Editions JP. **89:** Tyrolean Airways. **90/91:** Time Air. **96:** Austin J. Brown. **97:** UTA. **98:** CP Air. **99:** McDonnell Douglas Corporation. **100:** Austrian Airlines. **101:** Swissair. **102/103:** McDonnell Douglas Corporation. **104:** UTA. **105:** McDonnell Douglas Corporation. **108:** Air UK. **109:** Loganair. **110:** EMBRAER. **111:** Fokker-VFW. **112/113:** Pilgrim Airlines. **114:** Linjeflyg. **115:** KLM. **118:** Gulfstream Aerospace. **119:** Georges Schweikart via Editions JP. **120:** Editions JP. **121:** Prof. Johannes Zopp. **123:** Christian Laugier via Editions JP. **124:** Austin J. Brown. **129:** Aviation Letter Photo Service. **130/131:** Gulf Air. **132:** Lockheed. **133:** Delta Air Lines. **136:** Lockheed. **138:** Editions JP. **139:** Asahi Helicopter. **140:** All Nippon Airways. **142:** Piper. **143:** Saab-Fairchild. **144:** Olympic Airways. **147:** Sikorsky. **148:** Sikorsky. **151:** Swearingen Aircraft Corporation. **153:** Austin J. Brown. **154:** Austin J. Brown. **155:** British Midland Airways. **156:** Westland Helicopters. **157:** Ueli Klee via Editions JP.

Contents

Aérospatiale (Nord) 262 and Frégate/Mohawk 298 series

With the continuing problems that face the world's airlines in 1983, major operators staggering as the recession continues, it is not surprising that many small companies have failed to survive. Altair Airlines, once equipped with a fleet of Nord 262As, brought its operations to an end on 11 March 1982.

History and Notes

Nord-Aviation, later merged with Sud-Aviation to form Aérospatiale, built the first examples of the MH-260 light commuter transport which had been evolved by the well-known French designer Max Holste. The company then developed an improved version which it designated Nord 262. This introduced pressurized accommodation and was a conventional high-wing monoplane with a fuselage of circular cross-section, retractable tricycle landing gear, and power provided by two wing mounted Turboméca Bastan VIC turboprops in the Nord 262A; the designation Nord 262B applied to the first four production aircraft. Aérospatiale later developed an improved N.262C, named Frégate, with more powerful Bastan VII engines and new wingtips that increased wing span by 2 ft 3½ in (0.70 m); a generally similar military version was designated N.262D Frégate or Frégate D. Subsequently, in the USA, a Mohawk 298 version was planned by Mohawk Air Services. These conversions; carried out by Frakes Aviation and completed in 1978, replaced the Bastan engines in Allegheny Commuters Nord 262As with 1,180-shp (880-kW) Pratt & Whitney Aircraft of Canada PT6A-45 turboprops, and updated the aircraft by introducing improvements and new equipment. A total of 110 N.262s was built, of which rather less than a quarter now remain in service, the majority with Allegheny Commuter, Altair Airlines and Ransome Airlines.

Specification: Nord N.262A
Origin: France
Type: commuter transport
Accommodation: flight crew of 2; up to 29 passengers
Powerplant: two 1,080-shp (805-ekW) Turboméca Bastan VIC turboprops
Performance: maximum speed 239 mph (385 km/h); cruising speed 233 mph (375km/h); service ceiling 23,500 ft (7165 m); range with 26 passengers and no reserves 864 miles (1390 km)
Weights: empty operating 15,498 (7030 kg); maximum take-off 23,369 lb (10600kg)
Dimensions: span 71 ft 10¼ in (21.90 m); length 63 ft 3 in (19.28 m); height 20 ft 4 in (6.20 m); wing area 592.03 sq ft (55.00 m²)

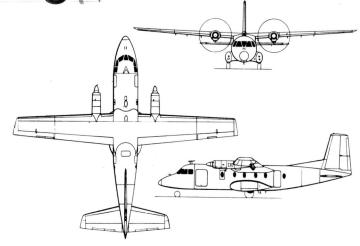

Aérospatiale (Nord) 262 Frégate

Once regarded as a 'DC-3 replacement', the Aérospatiale (Nord) 262 failed, as have so many other aspirants, to fulfil this role. Of the 110 that were built, only about 20 remained in service in 1983, the majority of them in the United States and 12 of this total being Mohawk 298 conversions by Frakes Aviation.

Aérospatiale SE 210 Caravelle

Of the total of 280 Caravelles that were built, just under 100 remained in use with some 24 operators in early 1983, the majority of them within Europe. The Caravelle 12 illustrated in this profile is no longer operated by Denmark's Sterling Airways, but six Caravelle 10Bs are still retained in its 16 aircraft fleet.

History and Notes

The Sud-Est (subsequently Aérospatiale) SE 210 Caravelle was the first turbojet-powered airliner of French design and construction. It introduced a then-unique powerplant installation with two engines in pods, one on each side of the rear fuselage, to ensure improved wing performance and a quieter cabin.

The SE 210-01 prototype (F-WHHH), powered by 10,000-lb (4536-kg) thrust Rolls-Royce Avon RA.26 turbojets, made its maiden flight on 27 May 1955, and Caravelle Is first entered service with SAS on 26 April 1959. Subsequent variants have included the generally-similar Caravelle Ia, Caravelle III with more powerful engines, Caravelle VI-N without and Caravelle VI-R with thrust-reversers, the Caravelle 10R with turbofan engines, a slightly-lengthened mixed passenger/cargo Caravelle 11B, a further 'stretched' Caravelle Super B, and the ultimate Caravelle 12 with a fuselage of still greater length, and performance improvements resulting from more powerful Pratt & Whitney JT8D engines. Production of all versions (including prototypes) totalled 280, major operators being Air France, Air Inter, Alitalia, Iberia, SAS, Sterling Airways and United Airlines. Just under 100 of these aircraft now remain in service.

Two variants were produced from Caravelle III airframes, a Caravelle VII prototype with General Electric CJ805-23C turbofans, and one given 12,200-lb (5534-kg) thrust Avon engines to serve as prototype of the Caravelle VI.

Specification: Aérospatiale Caravelle 12
Origin: France
Type: short/medium-range transport
Accommodation: flight crew of 3; up to 140 passengers
Powerplant: two 14,500-lb (6577-kg) thrust Pratt & Whitney JT8D-9 turbofans
Performance: maximum cruising speed at weight of 110,231 lb (50000 kg) 513 mph (826 km/h) at 25,000 ft (7620 m); range with maximum payload of 29,101 lb (13200kg) and no fuel reserves 2,153 miles (3465 km)
Weights: empty 65,036 lb (29500 kg); maximum take-off 127,868 lb (58000 kg)
Dimensions: span 112 ft 6 in (34.29 m); length 118 ft 10½ in (36.23 m); height 29 ft 7 in (9.02 m); wing area 1,579.12 sq ft (146.70 m²)

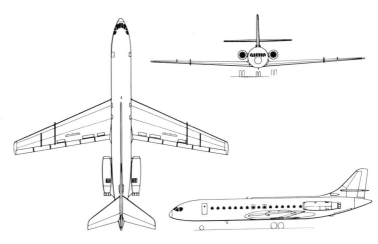

Aérospatiale Caravelle VI R

French airline Minerve (Compagnie Francaise de Transports Aériens) provides passenger and cargo charter operations in Africa, the Americas, Europe and the Middle East. For this work it uses a fleet of six aircraft, these including two Caravelle 6Ns, one 6R and a single Caravelle 10.

Aérospatiale/British Aerospace Concorde

F-BVFA, the Air France Concorde illustrated in this profile, was the fifth production example, first flown on 25 October 1975. It was this aircraft which the airline used to inaugurate its supersonic commercial services, initially operating between Paris and Rio de Janeiro via Dakar.

History and Notes

Numbered among the most famous civil airliners of aviation history, Concorde has the distinction of being the world's first supersonic transport (SST) to inaugurate scheduled passenger operations. These began on 21 January 1976 when Air France and British Airways began Paris-Rio de Janeiro and London-Bahrain services respectively. In 1983 the Concorde remains the only SST operating scheduled services, the Soviet Union's Tupolev Tu-144 having been withdrawn after a comparatively short operational life.

Development of SSTs was seen to be possible after flights by early supersonic bombers, and their potential time-saving for long-range flights suggested a big demand. After successful early testing, followed by demonstration and sales tours, this appeared to be confirmed by an order book totalling more than 70 aircraft from 12 major airlines. But by the time that services were inaugurated in 1976, escalating costs and anti-Concorde environmentalists had reduced the order book to nine Concordes for Air France and British Airways. Since then seven more production Concordes have been built, each manufacturer retaining one for development purposes and the two founder airlines each operating seven. Despite such limited production, Concorde has proved a supreme technological success.

Specification: Aérospatiale/British Aerospace Concorde
Origin: France/UK
Type: supersonic commercial transport
Accommodation: flight crew of 3; single-class layout for 100 passengers
Powerplant: four Rolls-Royce/SNECMA Olympus 593 Mk 610 turbojets, each developing 38,050-lb (17259-kg) thrust with afterburning
Performance: cruising speed for optimum supersonic range Mach 2.04 at 51,300 ft (15635 m), equivalent to 1,354 mph (2179 km/h); service ceiling 60,000 ft (18290 m); range with maximum payload and reserves 3,870 miles (6228 km)
Weights: empty operating 173,500 lb (78698 kg); maximum take-off 408,000 lb (185066 kg)
Dimensions: span 83 ft 10 in (25.55 m); length 203 ft 9 in (62.10 m); height 37 ft 5 in (11.40 m); wing area 3,856.0 sq ft (358.22 m²)

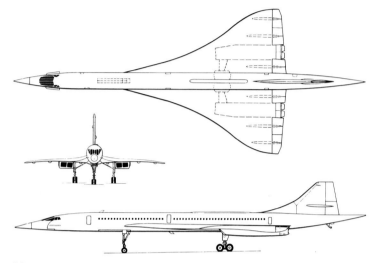

Aérospatiale/British Aerospace Concorde

Designed originally by Sud-Aviation in France and Bristol/British Aircraft Corporation in the UK, the Concorde SST was built by the successor companies to the above, Aérospatiale and British Aerospace respectively. Only a successful international collaboration could have produced such a complex aircraft.

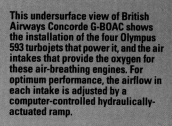

This undersurface view of British Airways Concorde G-BOAC shows the installation of the four Olympus 593 turbojets that power it, and the air intakes that provide the oxygen for these air-breathing engines. For optimum performance, the airflow in each intake is adjusted by a computer-controlled hydraulically-actuated ramp.

Aerospatiale/British Aerospace Concorde

The sixth production Concorde, which first flew on 5 November 1975 and entered service with British Airways on 21 January 1976 when it flew a service from London to Bahrain. The elegantly simple lines of the Concorde, optimized for an economical cruising speed of just over Mach 2, tend to disguise the extreme complexity, in both aerodynamics and systems, of this pioneering SST. Some indication of the sophisticated aerodynamic factors are indeed given by the modified ogival wing planform with its cambered leading edges, but the intricacies of the powerplant/fuel and electronics systems are not even suggested. The latter are the key to the effective operation of the aircraft, controlling the trim of the machine and the performance of the engines to suit exactly the relevant flight conditions. Though the nose is shown in the raised position, the visor is not extended.

British airways

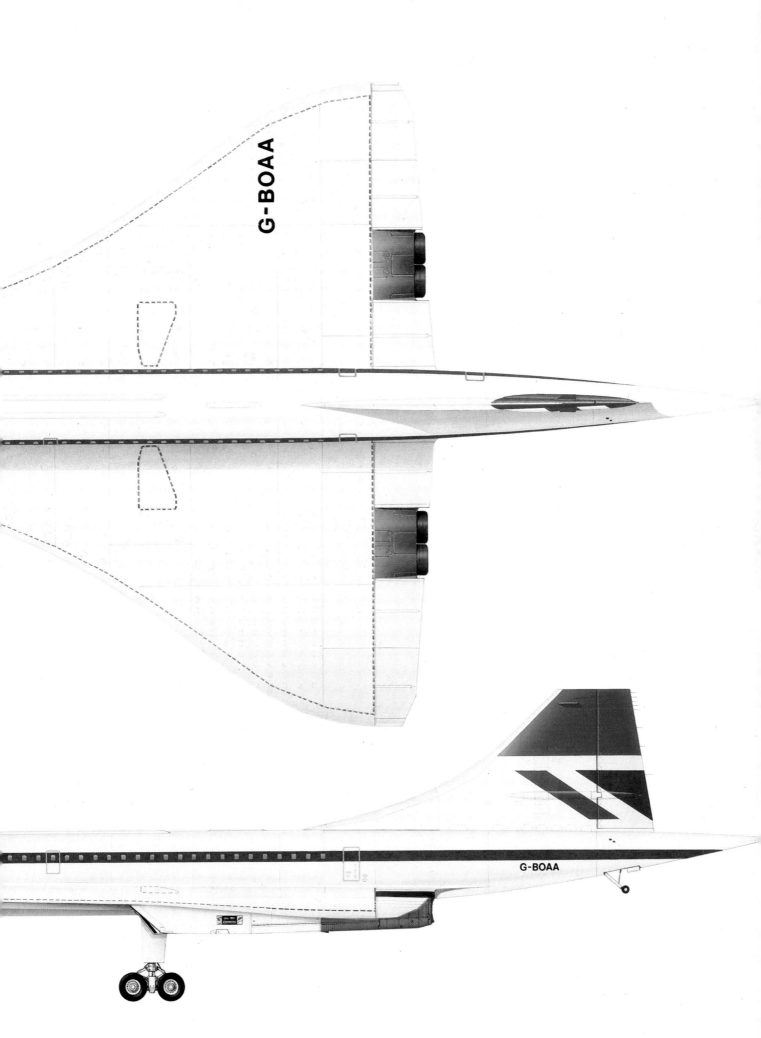

G-BOAA

G-BOAA

Aérospatiale SN 601 Corvette

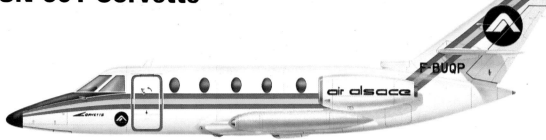

Air Alsace no longer has the SN.601 Corvette shown in this profile, but most of the 40 built remain in service in 1983. It may seem strange that an aircraft similar to many successful turbine-powered aircraft was built in such small numbers, but shows the importance of deciding aircraft capacity correctly.

History and Notes

First flown on 16 July 1970, the prototype SN 600 Corvette represented Aérospatiale's too-late entry into the lucrative business-jet market: this is reflected by the fact that, despite an attractive appearance and good performance, the Corvette was taken out of production in 1977 after only 40 examples had been built. Moreover, the Corvette was not only too late, but also just too small, as with accommodation for a crew of two and 14 passengers it was a large business aircraft but had inadequate capacity for most commuter airline operators.

A cantilever low-wing monoplane with swept wings and tail surfaces, the prototype was powered by two 2,200-lb (998-kg) thrust Pratt & Whitney Aircraft of Canada JT15D-1 turbofans, but production SN 601s had marginally more powerful JT15D-4s. The first SN 601 was flown on 20 December 1972, gaining French and FAA certification in May and September 1974 respectively, and the first delivery, to Air Alpes, was also made in the latter month. Although the majority of sales were to European operators, some went to the USA and Air National of San Jose, California had six in service in 1982. Proposed variants, none of which were built, included the 18-seat Corvette 200, a three-engined Corvette 300 and the SN 602 which would have been powered by 2,756-lb (1250-kg) thrust SNECMA/Turboméca Larzac 03 turbofans.

Specification: Aérospatiale SN 601
Origin: France
Type: light business/commuter transport
Accommodation: flight crew of 2; up to 14 passengers
Powerplant: two 2,500-lb (1134-kg) thrust Pratt & Whitney Aircraft of Canada JT15D-4 turbofans
Performance: maximum speed 472 mph (760 km/h) at 29,530 ft (9000 m); cruising speed 351 mph (565 km/h) at 39,000 ft (11900 m); service ceiling 41,010 ft (12500 m); range with maximum fuel 1,588 miles (2555 km)
Weights: empty 7,738 lb (3510 kg); maximum take-off 14,550 lb (6600 kg)
Dimensions: span 42 ft 2½ in (12.87 m); length 45 ft 4½ in (13.83 m); height 13 ft 10½ in (4.23 m); wing area 236.81 sq ft (22.00 m²)

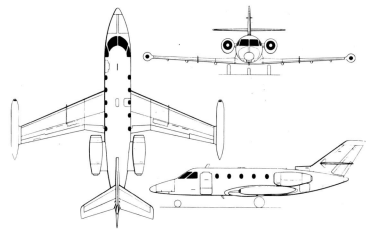

Aérospatiale SN 601 Corvette

Aérospatiale SN.601 Corvette 100s, the only production version of this attractive turbofan-powered light business and commuter transport, remain in service in 1983 with a number of charter operators. Sterling Airways of Denmark has two in service, its 14-passenger capacity suited to this operator's needs.

Aérospatiale SA 360 Dauphin series

The capability of Aérospatiale's Dauphin general-purpose helicopter soon became well known, and the introduction of the twin-turbine Dauphin 2 brought new sales activities. Far East interest is not confined to China; Japanese certification on 24 March 1982 for single-pilot IFR flight was followed by early deliveries.

History and Notes

Developed to replace the Aérospatiale Alouette III, the first SA 360 prototype (F-WSQL) flew initially on 2 June 1972. A general-purpose helicopter powered by a Turboméca Astazou turboshaft engine, the SA 360 incorporates in its design a four-blade main rotor, anti-torque tail *fenestron* or 'fan-in-fin', a horizontal stabilizer with endplate fins, a large vertical fin which can counter main rotor torque in cruising flight, and optional skid or wheel landing gear. Standard seating is for a crew of 1/2 and 9/8 passengers respectively, but a total of 14 persons can be carried in high-density seating. The SA 365C Dauphin 2 announced in 1973 is a twin-turbine version of the SA 360, the prototype (F-WVKE) flying first on 24 January 1975. It has since been superseded in production by the SA 365N Dauphin 2 of similar configuration but incorporating a high percentage of composite construction. All versions have IFR and VFR certification and a special aeromedical version is available. More than 320 Dauphins and Dauphin 2s have been ordered for civil and military use, including 90 for the US Coast Guard under the designation HH-65A Dolphin; China is licence-building a batch of 50 SA 365Ns.

Specification: Aérospatiale SA 365N Dauphin 2
Origin: France
Type: commercial general-purpose helicopter
Accommodation: flight crew of 1; up to 13 passengers
Powerplant: two 710-shp (529-kW) Turboméca Arriel IC turboshafts
Performance: maximum cruising speed 173 mph (278 km/h) at sea level; economic cruising speed 161 mph (259 km/h) at sea level; service ceiling 15,000 ft (4570 m); maximum range with standard fuel 548 miles (882 km)
Weights: empty equipped 4,398 lb (1995 kg); maximum take-off 8,488 lb (3850 kg)
Dimensions: main rotor diameter 39 ft 1¾ in (11.93 m); length, rotors turning 44 ft 2 in (13.46 m); height 13 ft 2 in (4.01 m); main rotor disc area 1,203.25 sq ft (111.78 m²)

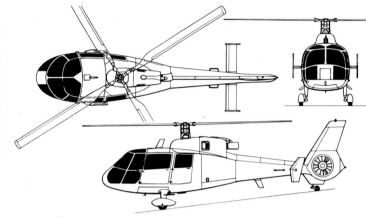

Aérospatiale SA 360 Dauphin

Within less than a year of the flight of the Dauphin 2 prototype, the first production aircraft (F-WZJJ) was used to set new helicopter records for Paris-London and return. On 8 February 1980 it carried six persons Paris-London in 1 hour 3 minutes 30 seconds, the return trip made in 1 hour 12 minutes 9 seconds.

Aérospatiale AS 350 Ecureuil/Astar

Not truly within the category of an airliner, the Aérospatiale AS 350 Ecureuil nevertheless offers invaluable service to both airlines and passengers, able to provide high-speed feeder services that eliminate the misery of road crawls. In London, as in many cities, such aircraft link major airports some miles apart.

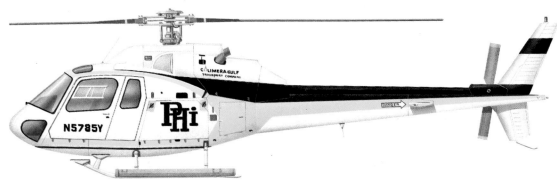

History and Notes

Designed as a successor to the Alouette, Aérospatiale's AS 350 Ecureuil (Squirrel) prototype (F-WVKH) was flown first on 27 June 1974. A lightweight general-purpose helicopter, its overall design is conventional, but it incorporates such features as a three-blade main rotor with glassfibre blades, the leading-edge of each blade protected by a stainless steel sheath, and Aérospatiale's Starflex advanced main rotor hub which is also of basic glassfibre construction. The two-blade anti-torque tail rotor has glassfibre blades, landing gear comprises simple steel tube skids, and power is provided by either a 616-shp (459-kW) Avco Lycoming LTS 101-600A.2 or a Turboméca Arriel turboshaft engine. An AS 355 Ecureuil 2 was introduced some five years later, the first prototype (F-WZLA) flown on 28 September 1979; it differs from the earlier version primarily by having twin-turbine power, provided by two 425-shp (317-kW) Allison 250-C20F turboshaft engines which enhance performance and load carrying capability. The AS 350 with Avco Lycoming engine is marketed in North America as the Astar, and for the same market the twin-turbine AS 355 is known as the Twinstar.

Specification: Aérospatiale AS 350B
Origin: France
Type: light general-purpose helicopter
Accommodation: pilot and four or five passengers
Powerplant: one 641-shp (478-kW) Turboméca Arriel turboshaft engine
Performance: maximum cruising speed 144 mph (232 km/h); service ceiling 15,000 ft (4575 m); range with maximum fuel, no reserves 435 miles (700 km)
Weights: empty 2,348 lb (1065 kg); maximum take-off internal load 4,300 lb (1950 kg)
Dimensions: main rotor diameter 35 ft 0¾ in (10.69 m); length 42 ft 7½ in (12.99 m); height 10 ft 4 in (3.15 m); main rotor disc area 966.09 sq ft (89.75 ²m)

Aérospatiale AS 350 Ecureuil

Almost 1,500 Ecureuil/Ecureuil 2 Astar/Twinstars have been sold to customers in some 31 countries. One version, designed in the US to meet requirements of the American Hospital Association, is equipped as an emergency ambulance with space for two stretchers, an attendant, and easily-accessible life-support equipment.

Airbus Industrie A300

One of the first three examples of the Airbus to be operated by Japan's Toa Domestic Airlines, JA8466 is an A300B2-203 which is powered by General Electric CF6-50C-2 engines. This powerplant combined with wing-root leading-edge Krueger flaps makes it suitable for operation from 'hot and high' airfields.

History and Notes

At the time that Boeing in the USA was finalizing its Model 747 wide-body transport, studies were initiated in the UK for a short-range civil airliner to carry 200 passengers, a size that BEA considered ideal for future requirements. In late 1965 eight European airlines met to consider proposals, but emphasized that a larger-capacity aircraft was needed in Europe's crowded airspace. Continuing discussions led to an alignment of Hawker Siddeley, Sud-Aviation (later Aérospatiale) and West Germany represented by Arbeitgemeinschaft Airbus (later Deutsche Airbus GmbH) as the design/production team. Fokker (Netherlands) and Construcciones Aeronauticas SA (Spain) joined later the company established in December 1970 as Airbus Industrie.

First to fly was the A300B1, on 28 October 1972, with the first A300B2, representing the basic production version, on 28 June 1973. The A300B2 entered service with Air France on 30 May 1974; it was soon found to be quiet in operation, economical, reliable, and easy to maintain and operate. What had once seemed a gamble became a major success story, with orders and options for A300s from 36 airlines in 29 countries totalling more than 300. Major operators include Air France (22), Eastern Air Lines (25), Indian Airlines (10), Lufthansa (11) and Thai International (10).

Specification: Airbus Industrie A300B4-200
Origin: International
Type: wide-body short/medium-range transport
Accommodation: flight crew of 3; up to 336 passengers
Powerplant: two 52,500-lb (23814-kg) thrust General Electric CF6-50C1 turbofans
Performance: maximum cruising speed 566 mph (911 km/h) at 25,000 ft (7620 m); long-range cruising speed 526 mph (847 km/h) at 31,000 ft (9450 m); range with 269 passengers, baggage and fuel reserves 3,340 miles (5375 km)
Weights: basic empty 176,000 lb (79832 kg); maximum take-off 363,763 lb (165000 kg)
Dimensions: span 147 ft 1¼ in (44.84 m); length 175 ft 11 in (53.62 m); height 54 ft 2¾ in (16.53 m); wing area 2,798.71 sq ft (260.00 m²)

Airbus Industrie A300B4

Europe's first true wide-body airliner, the Airbus Industrie A300B4-100 shown here is a longer-range development of the initial production version, the A300B2. Illustrated is HS-TGM of Thai Airways, named *Thepsatri*, one of a fleet of 10 used on a domestic network radiating out from Bangkok.

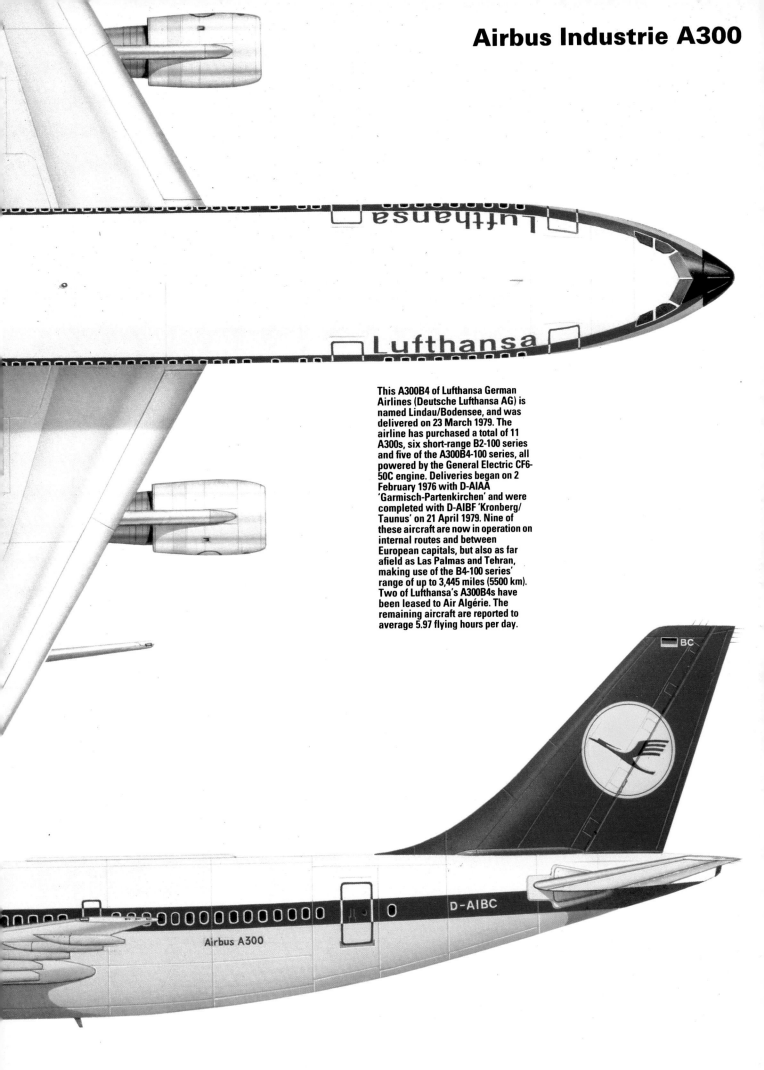

This A300B4 of Lufthansa German Airlines (Deutsche Lufthansa AG) is named Lindau/Bodensee, and was delivered on 23 March 1979. The airline has purchased a total of 11 A300s, six short-range B2-100 series and five of the A300B4-100 series, all powered by the General Electric CF6-50C engine. Deliveries began on 2 February 1976 with D-AIAA 'Garmisch-Partenkirchen' and were completed with D-AIBF 'Kronberg/Taunus' on 21 April 1979. Nine of these aircraft are now in operation on internal routes and between European capitals, but also as far afield as Las Palmas and Tehran, making use of the B4-100 series' range of up to 3,445 miles (5500 km). Two of Lufthansa's A300B4s have been leased to Air Algérie. The remaining aircraft are reported to average 5.97 flying hours per day.

Airbus Industrie A310

In addition to Swissair, with firm orders for 10 aircraft, major orders have been received from Lufthansa (25), KLM (10), Kuwait Airways (8), and VASP (9). It was anticipated that options which nearly double the 102 firm orders will be taken up later, as the A310 offers big economies to short haul operators.

History and Notes

To meet European and world airline requirements for a large-capacity short-range airliner, Airbus Industrie finalized the design and layout of the A310, which shares much component commonality with the A300. A decision to proceed with its development was made in July 1978 and the first of three prototypes (F-WZLH) made its maiden flight on 3 April 1982. Certification was gained in early 1983 with entry into service, initially with Lufthansa and Swissair, following shortly afterwards.

The A310 differs from the A300 by having a fuselage of reduced length to provide standard accommodation for 210 to 255 passengers with a maximum of 282 in high-density seating, a new advanced-technology wing of slightly reduced span, new and smaller horizontal tail surfaces, modified landing gear and new underwing pylons able to mount any of the alternative powerplants that are available from General Electric, Pratt & Whitney or Rolls-Royce. The initial production version has the designation A310-200, but an A310C-200 convertible, A310F-200 freighter and a long-range development known as the A310-300 are planned.

Orders and options for the A310 total 192 for service with 17 airlines, major firm orders received from Lufthansa (25), KLM (10), Swissair (10) and VASP (9).

Specification: Airbus Industrie A310-200
Origin: International
Type: wide-body short/medium-range transport
Accommodation: flight crew of 2; up to 282 passengers
Powerplant: two 48,000-lb (21772-kg) thrust Pratt & Whitney JT9D-7R4D1 turbofans
Performance: (estimated) maximum cruising speed 556 mph (895 km/h) at 30,000 ft (9145 m); long-range cruising speed 516 mph (830 km/h) at 37,000 ft (11280 m); range with maximum passengers and fuel reserves 2,865 miles (4610 km)
Weights: empty operating 169,525 lb (76895 kg); maximum take-off 305,560 lb (138,600 kg)
Dimensions: span 144 ft 0¼ in (43.90 m); length 153 ft 1½ in (46.67 m); height 51 ft 10½ in (15.81 m); wing area 2,357.37 sq ft (219.00 m²)

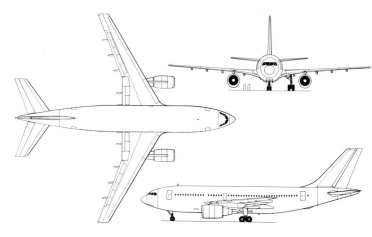

Airbus Industrie A310

The Airbus Industrie A310 Airbus, originally the A300B10, will seat normally 210 to 234 passengers in a fuselage that is 24 ft 7¾ in (7.51 m) shorter than the standard A300. French and German type certification was gained on schedule on 11 March 1983, with initial deliveries following to Lufthansa and Swissair.

Antonov An-12 'Cub'

Balkan Bulgarian Airlines is equipped exclusively with aircraft which originate from the Soviet Union. Shown in the profile is LZ-BAB, an Antonov An-12, which is the last of the type in service with the airline. More than 900 civil/military An-12s were built, some 250 remaining in airline service in 1983.

History and Notes

In 1955 the Antonov bureau began the design of a new civil airliner, a cantilever high-wing monoplane powered by four wing-mounted turboprops. Designated An-10 Ukraina in its initial version, first flown in March 1957, the aircraft accommodated 84 passengers, but the lengthened-fuselage An-10A could carry a maximum of 130 in a high-density layout. There was an extended development period before An-10s entered service with Aeroflot in 1959, the first scheduled service flown on 22 July. They remained in use until 1972.

A generally-similar An-12 military transport was developed simultaneously for the Soviet air force. Primary difference was a new upswept rear fuselage incorporating loading doors, plus a gunner's position in the tail, just below the trailing edge of the rudder. The An-12 became a standard freight and paratroop transport, an estimated 400 remaining in service with the Soviet air force in 1982. A civil version of the An-12 was introduced in 1965; it differs by having modified cargo doors beneath the rear fuselage that permit the use of a detachable ramp for loading and unloading; the provision of a pressurized cabin to seat 14, between the flight deck and cargo hold; and deletion of the tail gunner's position. These mixed passenger/cargo An-12s began to enter service with Aeroflot in February 1966, and more than half of this number remain in use.

Specification: Antonov An-12
Origin: USSR
Type: mixed passenger/cargo transport
Accommodation: flight crew of 3 or 4; up to 14 passengers
Powerplant: four 4,000-ehp (2983-ekW) Ivchenko AI-20K turboprops
Performance: maximum cruising speed 373 mph (600 km/h); normal cruising speed 342 mph (550 km/h) at 25,000 ft (7620 m); service ceiling 33,465 ft (10200 m); range with 22,046-lb (10000-kg) payload and fuel reserves 2,113 miles (3400 km)
Weights: normal take-off 119,050 lb (54000 kg); maximum take-off 134,482 lb (61000 kg)
Dimensions: span 124 ft 8 in (38.00 m); length 108 ft 7¼ in (33.10 m); height 34 ft 6½ in (10.53 m); wing area 1,310.0 sq ft (121.70 m²)

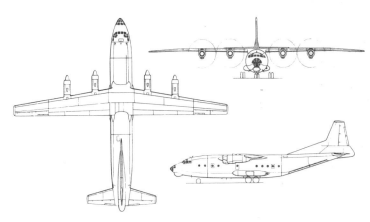

Antonov An-12

Iraqi Airways operate a fairly wide variety of aircraft, this Antonov An-12 one of six in service in early 1983. It is basically a freighter counterpart of the turboprop An-10, incorporating in the rear fuselage a ramp that can be lowered for the direct-in loading of vehicles or other kinds of large cargo.

Antonov An-14 'Clod'/An-28 'Cash'

Antonov's An-14M has since been replaced by a production version of this aircraft which has the designation An-28. It is to be built in Poland by WSK at Mielec and, by comparison with the An-14M, has fixed landing gear, larger tail surfaces, more powerful turboprop engines and a number of design refinements.

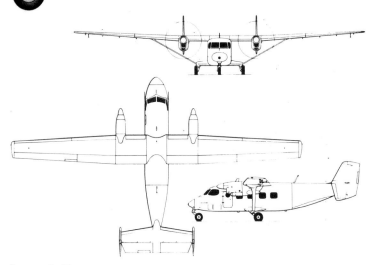

History and Notes

The Antonov An-14 was designed in 1957 as a STOL freighter and feederliner, with handling characteristics that would allow it to be flown by pilots with limited experience. However, its development was protracted, and it was not until 1965 that the type entered service. Production aircraft differed from the prototype by having a revised tail unit, modified wing planform, a lengthened nose, and clamshell doors incorporated in the rear fuselage.

The evolution of a turboprop development, designated initially An-14M, was reported in the early 1960s. However, it was not until September 1969 that the prototype made its first flight, then powered by 810-shp (604-kW) Isotov TVD-850 turboprops. A pre-production aircraft with the same powerplant followed, then redesignated An-28, but with the TVD-10B engines that were intended to power the first batch of production aircraft; it was flown first in April 1975. Designed to serve as a short-range transport, it has accommodation for a maximum of 20 passengers, but can be equipped alternatively in a variety of configurations. These can include agricultural, airmail, ambulance, cargo, firefighting, forest fire patrol, freight, geological survey, rescue and parachute training roles. In February 1978 it was announced that manufacture has been entrusted to PZL Mielec in Poland, and it has been planned that an initial batch of 15 An-28s will be built during 1983-4

Specification: Antonov An-28
Origin: USSR
Type: short-range light transport
Accommodation: flight crew of 2; up to 20 passengers
Powerplant: two 960-shp (716-kW) Glushenkov TVD-10B turboprops
Performance: cruising speed 208 mph (335 km/h) at 9,845 ft (3000 m); range with maximum payload 348 miles (560 km); range with maximum fuel 870 miles (1400 km)
Weights: empty 7,716 lb (3500 kg); maximum take-off 14,330 lb (6500 kg)
Dimensions: span 72 ft 5 in (22.07 m); length 42 ft 11¾ in (13.10 m); height 16 ft 1 in (4.90 m); wing area 427.34 sq ft (39.70 m²)

Antonov An-28

The Antonov An-14 Pchelka illustrated is one of the original version of this general purpose aircraft, which was powered by two 300-hp (224-kW) Ivchenko AI-14RF radial piston engines. It was superseded in 1969 by the AN-14M, introducing a fuselage lengthened by 7 ft 1 in (2.16 m) and turboprop powerplant.

Antonov An-22 'Cock'

Large fairings on each side of the An-22's fuselage house the main landing gear units when retracted, thus ensuring that they do not compromise cargo space in the main hold. So far as is known it is the only Soviet transport with the capability to airlift the Russian Army's 40-tonne T-62 battle tank.

History and Notes

In early 1962 the Antonov design bureau was given the task of designing and developing a long-range heavy transport. This presented more than average difficulty, for the aircraft was required to operate from and to the wide variety of terrains to be found throughout the Soviet Union. Antonov's design to meet these requirements resulted in a very substantial all-metal aircraft of high-wing monoplane configuration. Its large-capacity fuselage has an upswept rear section incorporating a loading ramp/door in its undersurface. Landing gear is of retractable tricycle configuration, but to allow for off-runway operations each main unit has three twin-wheel levered suspension units in tandem so that, with a twin-wheel nose unit, the aircraft has no fewer than 14 wheels to distribute its weight over the surface of the ground. Tyre pressures can be adjusted in flight, or on the ground, to give optimum performance for any airfield surface. It has been reported that operation into and from water-sodden grass fields is possible.

Designated An-22, the prototype was flown for the first time on 27 February 1965. Powerplant of production An-22s comprises four Kuznetsov turboprops. Accommodation is provided for a flight crew of five or six, and there is a small cabin in the forward fuselage, aft of the flight deck, seating 28 or 29 passengers. An-22s serve both with Aeroflot and the Soviet air force, which operate an estimated 40 and 50 respectively.

Specification: Antonov An-22
Origin: USSR
Type: long-range heavy transport
Accommodation: flight crew of 5 or 6; up to 29 passengers
Powerplant: four 15,000-shp (11186-kW) Kuznetsov NK-12MA turboprops
Performance: maximum speed 460 mph (740 km/h); cruising speed 348-398 mph (560-640 km/h); range with maximum payload of about 176,370 lb (80000 kg) 3,107 miles (5000 km)
Weights: empty operating 251,327 lb (114000 kg); maximum take-off 551,156 lb (250000 kg)
Dimensions: span 211 ft 3½ in (64.40 m); length 189 ft 7½ in (57.80 m); height 41 ft 1¼ in (12.53 m); wing area 3,713.7 sq ft (345.00 m²)

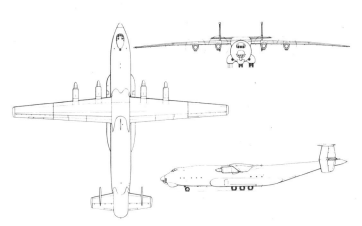

Antonov An-22

Among the world's truly giant aircraft, the Antonov An-22 Antheus came as something of a shock to aircraft manufacturers in the West when seen for the first time at the 1965 Paris Air Show. Used primarily in a cargo role by the Russian airline, Aeroflot, it never fails to gather an interested crowd.

Antonov An-24 'Coke'/An-26 'Curl'/An-30 'Clank'/ An-32 'Cline'

This Antonov An-24RV of TAROM, the national airline of Romania, is one of a total of about 24 of this version operated by the company. They differ from standard An-24s by the 1,984-lb (900-kg) thrust turbojet in the rear of the star board nacelle to improve engine starting, take-off and in-flight performance.

History and Notes

In late 1957 the Antonov bureau designed a 32/40-seat short/medium-range transport which it designated An-24, and the first of two prototypes was flown during April 1960. A cantilever high-wing monoplane, the An-24 has a wing incorporating high-lift devices to facilitate operations from a wide variety of airfields. Tricycle landing gear has twin wheels on each unit, with provision for varying tyre pressures in flight, and power is provided by two Ivchenko AI-24A turboprops.

Early production aircraft were delivered to Aeroflot in 1962, but it was September 1963 before the first 50-seat An-24Vs were used in revenue service. Subsequent versions include the An-24V Srs II with a variety of interiors; a similar An-24RV with an auxiliary turbojet to serve as an APU at remote airfields, or to improve performance; a specialized freighter with ventral freight door, designated An-24T or An-24RT with an auxiliary turbojet installed. An An-24P equipped to drop parachute-equipped firefighters was evaluated. Production of An-24s totalled about 1,000.

Closely related versions include the An-26 freighter with more powerful engines and large rear ramp/door; the An-30, basically a survey version of the An-26; and the An-32, a specialized 'hot-and-high' short/medium-range transport. This has 5,180-ehp (3863-kW) Ivchenko AI-20M turboprops for improved performance. India is reported to have ordered 95 with initial deliveries scheduled for 1983.

Specification: Antonov An-24V
Origin: USSR
Type: short-range transport
Accommodation: flight crew of 5; up to 50 passengers
Powerplant: two 2,550-ehp (1902-ekW) Ivchenko AI-24A turboprops
Performance: cruising speed 280 mph (450 km/h); service ceiling 27,560 ft (8400 m); range with maximum payload 342 miles (550 km)
Weights: empty 29,321 lb (13300 kg); maximum take-off 49,297 lb (22360 kg)
Dimensions: span 95 ft 9½ in (29.20 m); length 77 ft 2½ in (23.53 m); height 27 ft 3½ in (8.32 m); wing area 807.1 sq ft (74.98 m²)

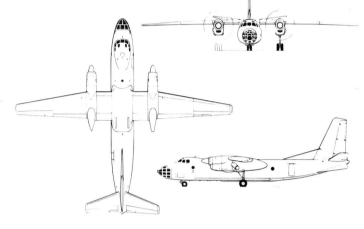

Antonov An-30

Cubana, the national airline of Cuba, is equipped almost exclusively (except for a single Britannia 300 in 1983) by aircraft which originate from the Soviet Union. Illustrated is an Antonov An-26, the freighter equivalent of the An-24 50-seat civil transport of which production ended during 1978.

Antonov An-72 'Coaler'

This side elevation of the new Antonov An-72 emphasizes the considerable anhedral on the outer wing panels. It also shows very well the positioning of the engines, high-set to avoid ingestion of debris when operating from rough strips, and the shape of the jetpipe which deflects the turbofan's efflux over the wing.

History and Notes

The first prototype of Antonov's An-72 twin-turbofan STOL freighter made its maiden flight on 22 December 1977. It adopts a similar STOL technique to that of the Boeing YC-14 military transport prototype, with the exhaust efflux from high-set turbofan engines ejected over the upper surface of the wing. Directed down and over large trailing-edge flaps, this airflow makes use of the so-called 'Coanda effect' to provide a significant increase in lift.

Other design features include tricycle landing gear with twin wheels on each unit, the main wheels in tandem; it is expected that production aircraft will have twin wheels on these mountings, giving a total of 10 wheels with low-pressure tyres to distribute the weight of the aircraft over a maximum surface area for operations from unprepared airfields. It is anticipated also that the special ramp/door developed for the An-26 will be incorporated: this hinges conventionally to serve as a ramp, but can be slid forward beneath the fuselage to make possible the on- or off-loading of cargo at truckbed height.

The main cabin, pressurized and air-conditioned, is intended primarily for freight, but has folding seats along the side walls for up to 32 passengers. It will also have provisions for use as an air ambulance, accommodating 24 stretchers and an attendant. Expected to enter service initially with Aeroflot, the An-72 clearly has military applications.

Specification: Antonov An-72 prototype
Origin: USSR
Type: twin-turbofan STOL transport
Accommodation: flight crew of 3; up to 32 passengers
Powerplant: two 14,330-lb (6500-kg) thrust Lotarev D-36 turbofans
Performance: maximum speed 472 mph (760 km/h); cruising speed 447 mph (720 km/h); service ceiling 36,090 ft (11000 m); range with maximum payload and fuel reserves 621 miles (1000 km)
Weights: maximum take-off 72,753 lb (33000 kg)
Dimensions: span 84 ft 9 in (25.83 m); length 87 ft 2½ in (26.58 m); height 27 ft 0¼ in (8.24 m); wing area 968.78 sq ft (90.00 m²)

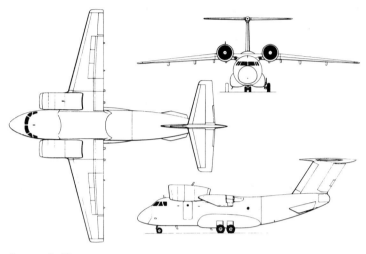

Antonov An-72

What are believed to be pre-production examples of the Antonov An-72 twin-turbofan STOL transport are currently in use with Aeroflot, presumably undergoing an extended programme of test and evaluation. However, CCCP-83966 (illustrated here) was first seen at the Paris Air Show during the summer of 1979.

Beech Model 18 and derivatives

The Beech Model 18 seen in this profile in the clean insignia of Air Cortez is a refurbished ex-military C-45H, powered by Pratt & Whitney R-985-AN-14B radials. Large numbers of Model 18s were given a new lease of life by such treatment; that of Air Cortez operates in Arizona, California and over the border to Mexico.

History and Notes

Some four years after its foundation in 1932, Beech Aircraft designed a twin-engine light transport designated Beech 18. First flown on 20 January 1937, the basic type was built to the extent of more than 9,000 examples before production of the H18 ended in the early 1970s. More than half were produced for military use during World War II, but both civil and ex-service aircraft have been used in large numbers by third-level airline and air-taxi operators. Very many still remain in service with such operators, especially in North and South America.

The Beech 18 is a conventional low-wing monoplane, the majority having retractable tailwheel landing gear, but optional tricycle gear could be installed on the Super H18 from September 1963. In addition to standard Beech Model 18s, a number of lengthened-fuselage and/or powerplant conversions were introduced by American manufacturers. These have included Dumod Corporation's nine-passenger Dumod I, and lengthened-fuselage 15-passenger Dumod Liner; Hamilton Aviation's 17-passenger turboprop-powered Westwind IISTD, a standard size turboprop-powered passenger/cargo Westwind III, and the larger-capacity lengthened-fuselage utility Westwind IV; Pacific Airmotive's 10-passenger Tradewind; and Volpar Inc's Super Turbo 18, a standard Beech 18 with turboprop powerplant and tricycle landing gear, and the 15-passenger turboprop-powered Turboliner.

Specification: Beech H18

Origin: USA
Type: light transport
Accommodation: flight crew of 2; up to 9 passengers
Powerplant: two 450-hp (336-kW) Pratt & Whitney R-985AN-14B radial piston engines
Performance: maximum speed 236 mph (380 km/h) at 4,500 ft (1370 m); economic cruising speed 185 mph (298 km/h) at 10,000 ft (3050 m); service ceiling 21,400 ft (6525m); maximum range with fuel reserves 1,530 miles (2462 km)
Weights: empty 5,845 lb (2651 kg); maximum take-off 9,900 lb (4491 kg)
Dimensions: span 49 ft 8 in (15.14 m); length 35 ft 2½ in (10.73 m); height 9 ft 4 in (2.84 m); wing area 360.70 sq ft (33.51 m²)

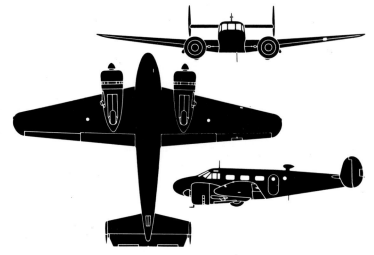

Beech Model 18 (C-45)

This Beech Model 18 of Eastern Caribbean is typical of so many to be found around the world. They share with the Douglas DC-3 robust and simple airframe construction, and reliable Pratt & Whitney radial piston engines that are unstressed by the loads with which they have to contend.

Beech Queen Air/Queen Airliner 70/80/88 series

Beech A65 Queen Air in service with Perimeter Airlines of Winnipeg, Manitoba. This Canadian operator provides scheduled passenger services with a fleet of medium-sized commuter/utility aircraft, and all but three of the 16 machines in use are of Beech manufacture, with Barons and Queen Airs predominating.

History and Notes

Flown for the first time on 22 June 1961, the Queen Air 80 was an improved version of the Queen Air 65 which had flown in August 1958. A conventional medium-size cabin monoplane, it had the low-set cantilever wing, wing-mounted engines and retractable tricycle landing gear of the Queen Air 65, but introduced a swept fin and rudder and replaced that aircraft's 340-hp (254-kW) Avco Lycoming powerplant by more powerful 380-hp (283-kW) engines from the same manufacturer. A developed A80 introduced in 1964 had increased wing span and a redesigned nose compartment. The Queen Air 70, which became available in 1968, combined the lower-powered engines of the Queen Air 65 with the A80 airframe.

Development of the Queen Air 80 continued with the B80 of 1965, an offshoot from this being the pressurized Queen Air 88. Easily distinguished from other members of the family by its round cabin windows, the Queen Air 88 was intended for operation at higher altitudes, providing increased economy in operation and greater comfort for its passengers. One other variant was the Queen Airliner B80, basically similar to the standard Queen Air B80 except for being equipped internally as an 11-seat commuter airliner. More than 500 of these various Queen Airs had been built by the time that the last two were delivered in 1977; fair numbers remain in use.

Specification: Beech Queen Air A80
Origin: USA
Type: business, commuter and utility transport
Accommodation: flight crew of 1 or 2 with 10 or 9 passengers respectively
Powerplant: two 380-hp (283-kW) Avco Lycoming IGSO-540-A1A flat-six piston engines
Performance: maximum speed 252 mph (406 km/h) at 11,500 ft (3505 m); cruising speed 230 mph (370 km/h) at 15,000 ft (4570 m); service ceiling 29,000 ft (8840 m); range 1,565 miles (2519 km)
Weights: empty 4,900 lb (2223 kg); maximum take-off 8,500 lb (3856 kg)
Dimensions: span 50 ft 3 in (15.32 m); length 35 ft 3 in (10.74 m); height 14 ft 8 in (4.47 m); wing area 293.86 sq ft (27.30 m²)

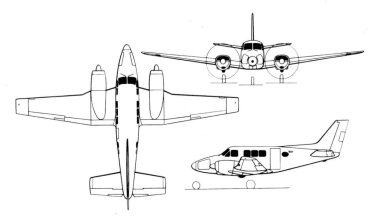

Beech Queen Air 80

The Beech Queen Air/Queen Airliner family is no longer in production, but many of the 500-plus that were built remain in service around the world. Their economy of operation, suitability for executive or commuter use, and average range of 1,000 miles (1609 km) is likely to keep them flying for some years.

Beech King Air 100/Super King Air 200

The Beech Super King Air 200 shown here was superseded in 1981 by the Super King Air B200 which has PT6A-42 turboprops to give improved altitude and cruise performance. Versions available are B200 basic, B200C with cargo door, B200T incorporating provisions for tiptanks and B200CT combining cargo door and tiptank provisions.

History and Notes

The King Air series was extended by Beech in 1969 with introduction of the King Air 100. By comparison with the King Air 90 it had a lengthened fuselage, larger tail control surfaces, twin-wheel main landing gear and more powerful engines. Improved A100s followed, of which five were supplied to the US Army as U-21Fs, these being the first turboprop-powered aircraft to be operated by that service. Current production version is the similar B100, first flown in March 1975, which introduced more powerful Garrett engines to improve performance.

FAA certification of the Super King Air 200 was gained in December 1973. It differs by having increased wing span, a higher cabin pressurization differential, a T-tail and 850-shp (634-kW) Pratt & Whitney Aircraft of Canada PT6A-41 turboprops. It was superseded in March 1981 by the B200 with similarly-powered PT6A-42 turboprops which give better performance and which is offered in optional Model 200C, 200T and 200CT utility configurations. A Maritime Patrol 200T is available, and multi-role Super King Airs have been supplied to the US Army under the designations C-12A, C-12C, and C-12D, RC-12D (ECM-equipped) and RU-21J (special missions). The US Navy/Marine Corps operate cargo/utility UC-12Bs with high-flotation landing gear and two Model 200Ts with similar landing gear serve with the French Institut Géographique National.

Specification: Beech King Air B100

Origin: USA
Type: light executive, freight or passenger transport
Accommodation: flight crew of 2; up to 13 passengers
Powerplant: two 550-eshp (410-ekW) Pratt & Whitney Aircraft of Canada PT6A-21 turboprops
Performance: maximum cruising speed 272 mph (438 km/h) at 12,000 ft (3660 m); service ceiling 28,100 ft (8565 m); range with maximum fuel and reserves 1,316 miles (2118 km)
Weights: empty 5,765 lb (2615 kg); maximum take-off 9,650 lb (4377 kg)
Dimensions: span 50 ft 3 in (15.32 m); length 35 ft 6 in (10.82 m); height 14 ft 3 in (4.34 m); wing area 293.94 sq ft (27.31 m²)

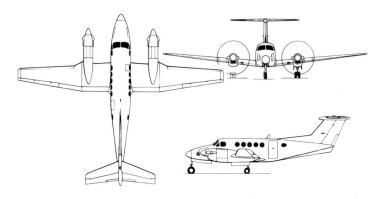

Beech Super King Air 200

Since the King Air 90 was first introduced in 1964, Beech has developed a family of King Airs which, in combined numbers, is approaching the 5,000 mark. Illustrated is a King Air B100, introduced in 1975, that is generally similar to its predecessors but has performance benefits from its 715-shp (533-kW) turboprops.

Beech Commuter C99

Mississippi Valley Airlines, a busy commuter operator based at La Crosse, Wisconsin, numbers seven Beech 99/C99 commuter aircraft in its fleet. They are kept fully occupied as feederliners, carrying large numbers of passengers to and from the many townships, some large, within easy reach of Chicago's O'Hare Airport.

History and Notes

The growth of commuter airlines prompted Beech in 1965 to embark on the design of an aircraft for this market. The resulting Model 99 Airliner, then the company's largest aircraft, was derived from the Queen Air family. Of the same general configuration, it had a lengthened fuselage to seat a maximum of 15 passengers. More powerful engines than those that powered the Queen Airs were required and initially 550-ehp (410-ekW) Pratt & Whitney Aircraft of Canada PT6A-20 turboprops were installed. Initial deliveries of production aircraft went to Commuter Airlines Inc. on 2 May 1968, and by the time production ended in late 1977, 164 aircraft had been delivered, most of them to customers in the USA.

On 7 May 1979 Beech announced the intention to re-enter the commuter airliner market with an updated version of the Model 99 Airliner, to be known as the Commuter C99, plus a new commuter 1900. A prototype of the C99 was produced by conversion of a B99 Airliner airframe, differing by some system changes, the installation of more powerful turboprop engines, and the incorporation as standard of some equipment which had previously been optional: the first C99 flew on 20 June 1980. Initial deliveries of production aircraft began on 30 July 1981 and some 20 aircraft were in service by early 1982.

Specification: Beech Commuter C99
Origin: USA
Type: commuter/cargo transport
Accommodation: flight crew of 2; up to 15 passengers
Powerplant: two Pratt & Whitney Aircraft of Canada PT6A-36 turboprops, each flat-rated at 715 shp (533 kW)
Performance: maximum speed 308 mph (496 km/h) at 8,000 ft (2440 m); cruising speed 287 mph (462 km/h) at 8,000 ft (2440 m); service ceiling 28,080 ft (8560 m); range with maximum fuel and reserves 1,048 miles (1,687 km)
Weights: empty operating 6,494 lb (2946 kg); maximum take-off 11,300 lb (5126 kg)
Dimensions: span 45 ft 10½ in (13.98 m); length 44 ft 6¾ in (13.58 m); height 14 ft 4¼ in (4.38 m); wing area 279.66 sq ft (25.98 m²)

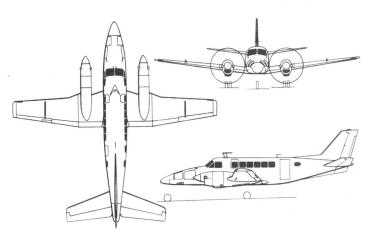

Beech Model 99

By comparison with the original Beech B99 Airliner, the new Commuter C99 has more powerful turboprop engines. These newer aircraft also incorporate a higher standard of installed equipment, and benefit from more developed systems that have been introduced on the newer generation of aircraft produced by Beech.

Beech 1900 Airliner

Note in this profile, and visible also in the accompanying picture, new auxiliary horizontal tail surfaces which have been added since the first prototype was flown. Named 'stabilons' by Beech, they are complemented by new vertical tail surfaces which have been added beneath the tips of the T-tail.

History and Notes

At much the same time that Beech was carrying out the first prototype conversion of a Commuter C99 in 1979, the company decided to initiate the design of a new commuter airliner, but one that would incorporate provisions for use in a convertible passenger/cargo role. In addition, the design of what was first named as the Commuter 1900 Airliner incorporates a pressurized fuselage for operation at higher altitudes than its predecessor. Following finalization of the design, the construction of two prototypes was started during 1981 and the first of these, which is to be used for performance evaluation and development, made its maiden flight on 3 September 1982. The second prototype is to be used for systems development, and a static test aircraft and a fuselage pressure cycle test aircraft are also being built. The first production aircraft was expected to fly during the spring of 1983, and it was planned to gain certification in the autumn with first production deliveries following shortly afterwards.

In configuration the 1900 Airliner is a cantilever low-wing monoplane with a fuselage structure intended for pressurization, retractable tricycle landing gear, a T-tail and power provided by two turboprop engines. The accommodation is heated and air-conditioned, seating 19 passengers as standard in an interior configured especially for commuter operations.

Specification: Beech 1900 Airliner
Origin: USA
Type: commuter airliner
Accommodation: flight crew of 2; up to 19 passengers
Powerplant: two Pratt & Whitney Aircraft of Canada PT6A-65B turboprops, each flat-rated at 1,000 shp (746 kW)
Performance: (estimated) maximum cruising speed 303 mph (488 km/h) at 10,000 ft (3050 m); service ceiling 30,000 ft (9145 m); range with maximum payload and fuel reserves 979 miles (1576 km)
Weights: (estimated) empty 8,500 lb (3856 kg); maximum take-off 15,245 lb (6915 kg)
Dimensions: span 54 ft 6 in (16.61 m); length 57 ft 9½ in (17.61 m); height 14 ft 10¾ in (4.54 m); wing area 303.0 sq ft (28.15 m²)

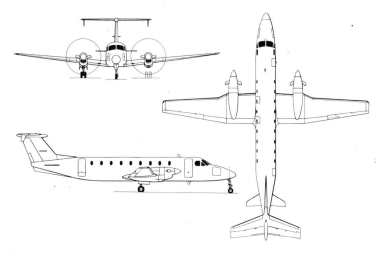

Beechcraft 1900

Renamed in 1983 as the Beechcraft 1900 Airliner, the development and production programme of this new commuter/cargo transport is progressing to schedule. At that time the first two prototypes had flown, the second on 30 November 1982, and the first production aircraft was nearing completion.

Bell Model 212 Twin Two-Twelve

The commercial Twin Two-Twelve helicopter derives from the company's long established military Iroquois, the reliability of its proven airframe enhanced by incorporation of a Twin Pac twin turbine powerplant. As an alternative to its passenger complement, it can lift an externally suspended load of 5,000 lb (2268 kg).

History and Notes

On 1 May 1968 Bell Helicopters announced negotiations with the Canadian government and Pratt & Whitney Aircraft of Canada covering the development of a new helicopter based on the Model 205/UH-1H Iroquois, of which examples were serving with the Canadian Armed Forces (CAF). These were each powered by an Avco Lycoming T53 turboshaft engine, and the CAF considered that twin turboshaft engines would offer benefits. Thus began development of a military Bell Model 212, its main feature a new PT6T Turbo Twin Pac powerplant, comprising two turboshaft engines arranged to drive a single output shaft. In the event of a turbine failure, sensing torquemeters signal the other unit to full power to provide true engine-out capability. Initial deliveries of Model 212s were made to the USAF in 1970 under the designation UH-1N, and the first CUH-1H (later CH-135) for the CAF was handed over on 3 May 1971.

A 14-passenger commercial Twin Two-Twelve was developed simultaneously, differing primarily in cabin furnishing and avionics equipment. The enhanced safety offered by the Twin Pac powerplant resulted in sales to many operators providing support to offshore gas/oil prospecting/production companies and air taxi operators. Major operators include Abu Dhabi Helicopters, Bristow Helicopters, Helikopter Service A/S and Okanagan Helicopters.

Specification: Bell Model 212 Twin Two-Twelve

Origin: USA
Type: commercial transport helicopter
Accommodation: pilot and up to 14 passengers
Powerplant: one Pratt & Whitney Aircraft of Canada PT6A-3B Turbo Twin Pac flat-rated to 1,290 shp (962 kW)
Performance: maximum cruising speed 142 mph (229 km/h) at sea level; service ceiling 14,200 ft (4330 m); range with standard fuel at sea level, no reserves 261 miles (420 km)
Weights: empty 6,143 lb (2786 kg); maximum take-off 11,200 lb (5080 kg)
Dimensions: main rotor diameter 48 ft 2¼ in (14.69 m); length, rotors turning 57 ft 3¼ in (17.46 m); height 14 ft 10¼ in (4.53 m); main rotor disc area 1,809.0 sq ft (168.06 m²)

Bell Model 212 Twin Two-Twelve

Bristow Helicopters in the UK number many Bell 212s in its fleet, operated in a variety of roles. The flexibility of this helicopter appealed also to the People's Republic of China, which acquired eight Two-Twelves in 1979. These were procured to support the development of natural resources and energy.

Bell Model 222

The unique capability of the helicopter has proved invaluable in providing support on many different operations. Helikopter Service AS of Oslo has used Bell helicopters since its formation in 1956, and this Model 222 is just one of 17 Bell types in the 40-plus fleet that is on call around the clock.

History and Notes

Bell Helicopters announced in April 1974 the company's intention to develop a new commercial helicopter designated Model 222, then described as the first light twin-turbine commercial helicopter to be built in the USA. The construction of five prototypes was initiated, the first of these flying on 13 August 1976, and their use in an accelerated development programme resulted in FAA certification in VFR configuration on 20 December 1979.

The Model 222 benefits from new-technology features developed at an earlier date for both civil and military helicopters; this includes Bell's nodal suspension system which results in a reduction of more than 70 per cent in rotor-induced vibration. The airframe incorporates a short-span cantilever sponson on each side, its aerofoil section providing some lift in forward flight and serving also to house the main units of the retractable tricycle landing gear. An improved Model 222B was introduced in early 1982 with a number of dimensional changes, including a 42 ft 0 in (12.80 m) diameter main rotor. Powered by uprated engines, the Model 222B has a maximum take-off weight of 8,250 lb (3742 kg). A total of about 60 Model 222s had been delivered by the spring of 1982, with initial deliveries going to Petroleum Helicopters and Schiavone Construction.

Specification: Bell Model 222
Origin: USA
Type: light commercial helicopter
Accommodation: flight crew of 1 or 2 and a maximum of 9 or 8 passengers respectively
Powerplant: two Avco Lycoming LTS 101-650C-3 turboshafts, each with a take-off rating of 620 shp (462 kW)
Performance: economic cruising speed 153 mph (246 km/h) from sea level to 4,000 ft (1220 m); service ceiling 20,000 ft (6095 m); range with maximum fuel and reserves 325 miles (523 km)
Weights: empty equipped 4,860 lb (2204 kg); maximum take-off 7,850 lb (3561 kg)
Dimensions: main rotor diameter 39 ft 9 in (12.12 m); length of fuselage 36 ft 0¼ in (10.98 m); height 11 ft 6 in (3.51 m); main rotor disc area 1,241.0 sq ft (115.29 m²)

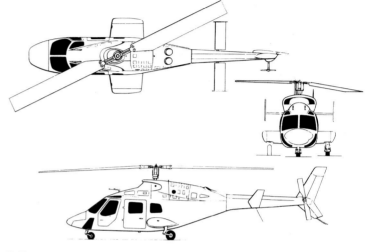

Bell Model 222

One of the twin-turbine Bell Model 222s delivered in 1981 was the 25,000th helicopter to be built by the company. This figure emphasizes Bell's experience in rotary-wing design and two Model 222s in use with London's Metropolitan Police are regarded as among the most advanced police helicopters in the world.

This picture emphasizes some design features of a modern helicopter. They include a small and unlubricated rotor head, twin turbines mounted over the cabin, retractable landing gear with the main units housed in sponsons that contribute some lift, and increased tail surfaces to improve stability and offset rotor torque.

Bell Model 214ST

The 18-passenger capacity of Bell's Model 214ST helicopter makes it an interesting proposition to many operators. British Caledonian Helicopters was one of the first companies to order the type, its capacity and fully-laden range making it attractive for use on the company's offshore operations to gas/oil platforms.

History and Notes

In late 1970 Bell Helicopters built a prototype identified as the Model 214 Huey Plus. It was basically an improved UH-1H Iroquois with increased power and structural strengthening for operation at a higher gross weight. From it was developed a 16-seat utility Model 214A which, as a result of negotiations concluded between the government of Iran and Bell in 1975, was expected to become the first production of an indigenous aircraft industry to be established in Iran. The revolution of early 1979 and changed national policies brought an end to this plan, but Bell continued development of this helicopter as the Model 214ST commercial transport.

A prototype was flown in February 1977, and was followed by three pre-production aircraft in 1978. The first was flown on 21 July 1979, and certification was gained on 16 February 1982. Initial deliveries of production aircraft began shortly afterwards, the first going to Petroleum Helicopters Inc. Other early deliveries are to Aramco in Saudi Arabia, British Caledonian Helicopters, Petrolair in Greece and the Venezuelan air force.

During development the gross weight has been increased, making it possible to carry a maximum of 18 passengers, and in 1983 optional tricycle landing gear became available to replace the standard skids, required by operators who use airports where taxiing is essential.

Specification: Bell Model 214ST
Origin: USA
Type: commercial transport helicopter
Accommodation: flight crew of 2; up to 18 passengers
Powerplant: two 1,625-shp (1212-kW) General Electric CT7-2A turboshafts
Performance: normal cruising speed 159 mph (256 km/h) at sea level; service ceiling on single engine 7,000 ft (2135 m); range with standard fuel and no reserves 501 miles (806 km)
Weights: empty equipped 9,481 lb (4300 kg); maximum take-off 17,500 lb (7938 kg)
Dimensions: main rotor diameter 52 ft 0 in (15.85 m); length, rotors turning 62 ft 2¼ in (18.95 m); height 15 ft 10½ in (4.84 m); main rotor disc area 2,124.0 sq ft (197.32 m²)

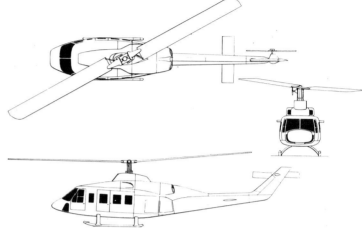

Bell Model 214ST

The rotor system of Bell's Model 214ST incorporates new technology glassfibre blades, a lubrication-free main rotor head, and the most developed form of the company's nodal suspension system to isolate the cabin from rotor vibration. Such features enhance the reliability of the 214ST for offshore operations.

Boeing Model 707

This 707-320 of Sudan Airways, ST-AFA *Blue Nile*, is one of two long-range aircraft which maintain the company's international 'Blue Nile' route from Khartoum to London, via Athens, Rome and Frankfurt. It is complemented on this service by the 707-320 ST-AFB, which carries the name *White Nile*.

History and Notes

Flown first on 15 July 1954, Boeing's Model 367-80 prototype was used initially as a military demonstrator. With a Boeing-designed inflight-refuelling boom it was able to show the USAF the potential of a turbojet-powered inflight-refuelling tanker. Boeing won an initial contract for 29 KC-135A tanker/transports and eventually built more than 800 aircraft under basic C-135 and C-137 designations.

The 'Dash-80' was then equipped as a civil demonstrator, gaining an order from Pan American for six Model 707-120s on 13 October 1955. The airline operated its first service on 26 October 1958, and when production ended in late 1980 967 had been delivered. They included the Model 707-020 (original designation of the Model 720), the Model 707-120, Model 707-120B (with turbofans) and Model 707-220 domestic models; and the Model 707-320, Model 707-320B (turbofans), Model 707-320C cargo or mixed cargo/passenger, and Model 707-420 (Rolls-Royce Conway powered) long-range versions. Final production version was the Model 707-320C Convertible, multi-purpose aircraft carrying up to 219 passengers. Powerplants varied from the 9,500-lb (4309-kg) thrust Pratt & Whitney JT3P turbojets of the prototype to the 19,000-lb (8618-kg) thrust turbofans of the final version. The superb Model 707 served with most of the world's major airlines and more than 300 remain in use.

Specification: Boeing 707-320C Convertible
Origin: USA
Type: commercial transport
Accommodation: flight crew of 3 or 4; up to 219 passengers
Powerplant: four 19,000-lb (8618-kg) thrust Pratt & Whitney JT3D-7 turbofans
Performance: maximum cruising speed 605 mph (974 km/h); economic cruising speed 550 mph (885 km/h); service ceiling 39,000 ft (11885 m); range with maximum fuel, reserves and 147 passengers 5,755 miles (9262 km)
Weights: empty operating, passenger 146,400 lb (66406 kg); maximum take-off 333,600 lb (151318 kg)
Dimensions: span 145 ft 9 in (44.42 m); length 152 ft 11 in (46.61 m); height 42 ft 5 in (12.93 m); wing area 3,050.0 sq ft (283.35 m²)

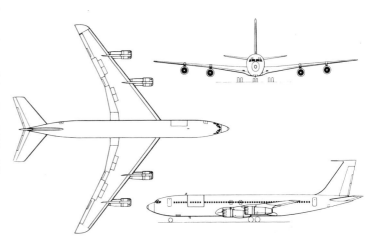

Boeing 707-320C

Avianca of Colombia, which is the oldest airline in the Americas (1919), has an all-Boeing fleet of transports. This 707-320 Intercontinental is typical of these superb airliners, which for almost a quarter of a century have provided operators around the world with a truly reliable international transport.

Boeing Model 707

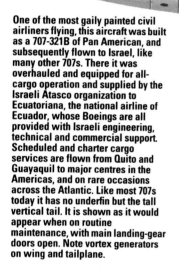

One of the most gaily painted civil airliners flying, this aircraft was built as a 707-321B of Pan American, and subsequently flown to Israel, like many other 707s. There it was overhauled and equipped for all-cargo operation and supplied by the Israeli Atasco organization to Ecuatoriana, the national airline of Ecuador, whose Boeings are all provided with Israeli engineering, technical and commercial support. Scheduled and charter cargo services are flown from Quito and Guayaquil to major centres in the Americas, and on rare occasions across the Atlantic. Like most 707s today it has no underfin but the tall vertical tail. It is shown as it would appear when on routine maintenance, with main landing-gear doors open. Note vortex generators on wing and tailplane.

ECUATORIANA
JET CARGO

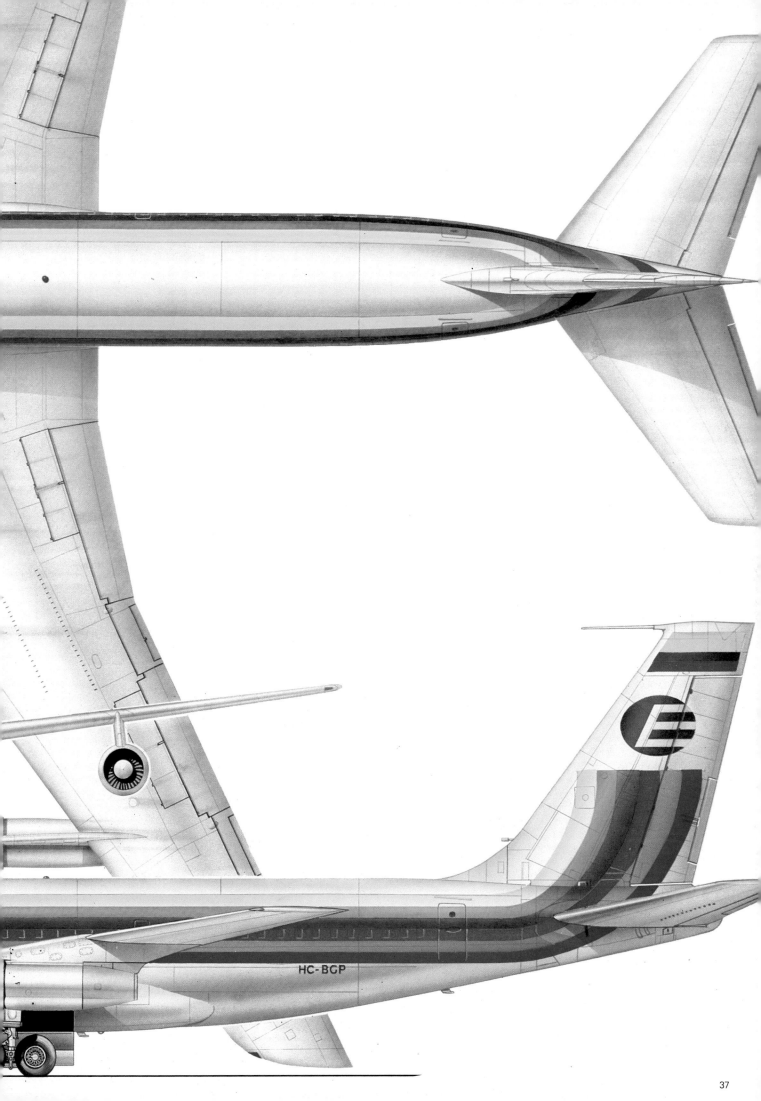

HC-BGP

Boeing Model 720

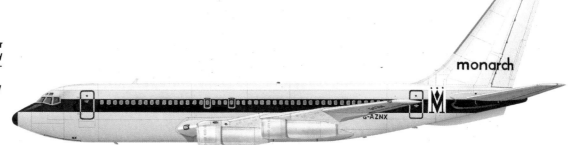

Monarch Airlines, British inclusive-tour and world-wide charter operator based at Luton Airport, relies heavily upon its five Boeing 720Bs on a year-round basis. They are due to be supplemented and, presumably, duly replaced by Boeing 737s and new-generation Boeing 757s which the airline had on order in 1982.

History and Notes

The early success of the Boeing 707 led to development of an intermediate range version designated initially Model 707-020. Similar externally to the Model 707-120, the Model 707-020 introduced aerodynamic refinements and, because there were also powerplant and structural changes, the designation Model 720 was allocated.

The major aerodynamic refinements were to the wing leading edge, which also gained four additional segments of flaps, making it the first of the family to have full-span leading-edge flaps. Fuselage length was reduced by 7 ft 9 in (2.36 m) in comparison with that of the Models 707-120/-220 which, together with a reduced fuel load made it possible to lighten the structure. Typical accommodation was for 38 first and 74 tourist-class passengers. The basic model, powered by four 12,500-lb (5670-kg) thrust Pratt & Whitney JT3C-7 turbojets, flew for the first time on 23 November 1959 and entered service, initially with United Airlines, on 5 July 1960. It was followed by the improved Model 720B, flown on 6 October 1960 and first used by American Airlines on 12 March 1961.

However, there was only limited demand for the smaller-capacity Model 720/720Bs, and production ended during 1969 after a total of 154 had been delivered. Just over a third of this number now remains in service, the major operator being Middle East Airlines.

Specification: Boeing Model 720B
Origin: USA
Type: intermediate-range commercial transport
Accommodation: flight crew of 4; up to 165 passengers
Powerplant: four 18,000-lb (8165-kg) thrust Pratt & Whitney JT3D-3 turbofans
Performance: maximum cruising speed 611 mph (983 km/h) at 25,000 ft (7620 m); economic cruising speed 557 mph (896 km/h) at 40,000 ft (12190 m); service ceiling 42,000 ft (12800 m); range with maximum payload and no reserves 4,155 miles (6687 km)
Weights: empty operating 112,883 lb (51203 kg); maximum take-off 234,000 lb (106141 kg)
Dimensions: span 130 ft 10 in (39.88 m); length 136 ft 9 in (41.68 m); height 41 ft 6½ in (12.66 m); wing area 2,521.0 sq ft (234.20 m²)

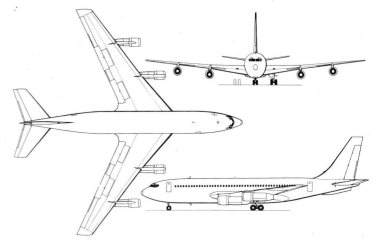

Boeing Model 720B

An intermediate-range development of the Boeing 707 was known initially as the Model 707-020. To avoid confusion between this and the 707-120, and also to reflect the introduction of structural changes, the designation Model 720 was allocated. When established in 1973, Air Malta acquired a fleet of five 720Bs.

Boeing Model 727

Better known to old enthusiasts as Allegheny Airlines, the name USAir was adopted to emphasize the fact that this carrier had become a significant national carrier. It numbers among its 100-plus fleet of airliners 16 727s, including five of these Advanced 727-200s that will be the final production version.

History and Notes

Numbered among the world's classic airliners, Boeing's short/medium-range Model 727 was first announced on 5 December 1960. A new advanced wing was developed to cater for low-speed/short-field operations and to provide economic low-altitude/high-speed cruising capability; it brought also selection of a rear-mounted engine installation to ease wing development. The upper lobe of the Model 707 fuselage was adopted, but a new reduced-height lower fuselage was used as less cargo/baggage space was needed. The design incorporated two important features: a ventral airstair and an auxiliary power unit, allowing independent operation at small airports.

The first Model 727-100 was flown on 9 February 1963, Eastern Air Lines first using Model 727s in service on 1 February 1964. This basic version was followed by a convertible cargo/passenger Model 727-100C and a quick-change cargo or passenger Model 727-100QC, both available in 1966. A similar Model 727-200, differing by having a fuselage lengthened by 10 ft (3.05 m), entered service in 1967. From it was developed the current higher gross weight Advanced 727-200 and all-cargo Advanced 727-200F, introduced in 1973 and 1981 respectively. In mid-1982 a total of 1,823 Model 727s of all versions had been ordered, of which almost 1,700 serve with some 100 airlines. Major operators, each with over 100 aircraft, are American Airlines, Delta Air Lines and United Airlines.

Specification: Boeing Advanced 727-200
Origin: USA
Type: commercial airliner
Accommodation: flight crew of 3; up to 189 passengers
Powerplant: three 14,500-lb (6577-kg) thrust Pratt & Whitney JT8D-9A turbofans
Performance: maximum cruising speed 599 mph (964 km/h) at 24,700 ft (7530 m); economic cruising speed 542 mph (872 km) at 30,000 ft (9145 m); typical range with fuel reserves 2,303 miles (3,706 km)
Weights: empty operating 100,000 lb (45,359 kg); maximum take-off 209,500 lb (95028 kg)
Dimensions: span 108 ft 0 in (32.92 m); length 153 ft 2 in (46.69 m); height 34 ft 0 in (10.36 m); wing area 1,700.0 sq ft (157.93 m²)

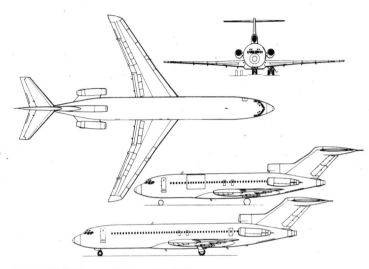

Boeing 727-200 (upper side view: 727-100C)

Most extensively-built turbine-powered airliner in the world, with more than 1,800 delivered, production of the Boeing 727 is scheduled to end in 1984. Iberia is but one of 100 operators that are likely to utilize their 727 fleet for some years to come, the one here (EC-DCC) an Advanced 727-200.

This short/medium-range Boeing 727 of Trans World Airlines is of the variant known as an Advanced 727-200. Powerful engines provide a maximum take-off weight of 209,500 lb (95028 kg) and it carries an on-board computer that provides information to the crew for optimum management of flight performance and fuel economy.

Boeing Model 737

US carrier Air Florida operates a large fleet of these Advanced 737-200s and has a considerable number on order. Sales have always trailed behind the 727, but with more than 1,000 ordered and a new 737-300 planned for delivery in late 1984 this short-range member of the Boeing family may yet eclipse the 727.

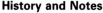

History and Notes

Boeing announced in 1965 the Model 737 short-range transport. It incorporated a wing similar to the Model 727, a fuselage basically that of the Model 727 but without the airstair and sized for a maximum 115 passengers, and a tail similar to that of the Model 707. A first Model 737-100 flew on 9 April 1967, Lufthansa using the type first on 10 February 1968. It was followed by a developed Model 737-200 with a lengthened fuselage for up to 130 passengers. United Airlines introduced this version on 29 April 1968; a year later Model 737-200C convertible and Model 737-200QC quick-change models became available. New versions announced in 1971 included the Advanced 737-200, available also in -200C and -200QC variants, all equipped to operate from airfields as short as 4,000 ft (1220 m); they remain in production in 1983. Business/executive versions have included the Model 737-200 Business Jet, Advanced 737-200 Business Jet and current Advanced 737-200 Executive Jet. Higher gross weight versions are available for longer-range use.

In 1980 work began to develop a larger-capacity Model 737-300. It will incorporate refinements to the wing, a lengthened fuselage for a maximum 149 passengers, and new-generation fuel-efficient turbofan engines. Its first flight is planned for early 1984. Orders for all versions comfortably exceed 1,000 and more than 800 are in service with some 100 airlines. The total includes 19 Model 737-200s modified as T-43A navigation trainers for the USAF.

Specification: Boeing Advanced 737-200
Origin: USA
Type: commercial transport
Accommodation: flight crew of 2; up to 130 passengers
Powerplant: two 16,000-lb (7257-kg) thrust Pratt & Whitney JT8D-17A turbofans
Performance: maximum cruising speed 532 mph (856 km/h) at 33,000 ft (10060 m); range with 115 passengers and reserve fuel 2,136 miles (3438 km)
Weights: empty operating 61,630 lb (27955 kg); maximum take-off 128,100 lb (58105 kg)
Dimensions: span 93 ft 0 in (28.35 m); length 100 ft 2 in (30.53 m); height 37 ft 0 in (11.28 m); wing area 980.0 sq ft (91.04 m²)

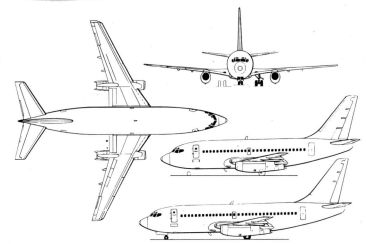

Boeing 737-200 (upper side view: 737-100)

As in the case of the Boeing 727, Advanced versions of the Boeing 737 have been introduced. This Advanced 737-200 of Air Europe (G-BMHG *Adam*) is one of the eight all-737 fleet operated by this busy UK holiday charter airline which, in 1983, was providing a high standard of service to some 30 European destinations.

Japan's Southwest Air Lines, based on Okinawa, provides island-linking services throughout the Ryukyu Archipelago which stretches out from Japan across the western Pacific. Its fleet of some 16 aircraft includes five Advanced 737-200s, their overall capability and short-field performance ideal for such operations.

If the name Flying Tigers means nothing to you, the absence of standard cabin windows from this Model 747 should pin-point the fact that it is a cargo rather than passenger carrier. A Model 747-200F Freighter, it has a nose loading door and a cargo handling system that enables two men to load it to capacity in 30 minutes.

Boeing Model 747/747SR

Avianca's 747 illustrated here (HK2000 *Eldorado*) is also one of the original -100 versions of which 167 were built. The true heavyweight is the 747-200B introduced in 1971, which is available with a variety of powerplants. It can be operated at a maximum take-off weight of 833,000 lb (377842 kg), about 378 tonnes.

History and Notes

Boeing announced simultaneously on 13 April 1966 that it was to begin manufacture of a new wide-body long-range transport, and that Pan American had concluded a $525 million contract for 25 of these aircraft and spares. Its dimensions and capacity fired the imagination of journalists who soon dubbed it 'jumbo jet', a name to become better known than the official Model 747. No prototype was built and the first production aircraft was flown on 9 February 1969; Pan American inaugurated its first New York-London service with the type on 22 January 1970.

The Model 747 has a wing incorporating features developed for other members of the family, tricycle landing gear that has four four-wheel main bogies, and a cabin 187 ft (57 m) long and 20 ft 1½ in (6.13 m) wide: in the initial Model 747-100 this provided accommodation for a maximum of 490 passengers. Currently available versions include the Model 747-100B with strengthened structure; the similar-capacity Model 747-200B operating at higher weights; the Model 747SR short-range version of the Model 747-100B; the Model 747-200B Combi for all-passenger or passenger/cargo operations; the Model 747-200C Convertible for all-passenger, all-cargo or combinations of both; and the all-cargo Model 747-200F Freighter.

Orders for all versions of the Model 747 are approaching the 600 mark; major operators include Air France, British Airways, Japan Airlines, Northwest Airlines and Pan American.

Specification: Boeing 747-200B
Origin: USA
Type: heavy commercial transport
Accommodation: flight crew of 3; up to 516 passengers, this including 32 on upper deck
Powerplant: four 54,750-lb (24834-kg) thrust Pratt & Whitney JT9D-7R4G2 turbofans
Performance: maximum speed 602 mph (969 km/h) at 30,000 ft (9145 m); cruise ceiling 45,000 ft (13715 m); range with fuel reserves and 452 passengers 6,563 miles (10,562 km)
Weights: empty operating 382,000 lb (173272 kg); maximum take-off 833,000 lb (377842 kg)
Dimensions: span 195 ft 8 in (59.64 m); length 231 ft 10 in (70.66 m); height 63 ft 5 in (19.33 m); wing area 5,500.0 sq ft (510.95 m²)

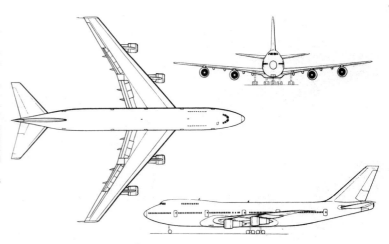

Boeing 747-200B

Queen of Boeing's family of turbine-powered airliners, this Model 747-100 of Wardair Canada (CF-DJC *Phil Garrett*) represents the initial production version which first entered service in January 1970. The -100 remains available in 1983, as the 747-100B with a strengthened structure, or short-range 747SR.

For anyone who has never travelled by or stood close to a Boeing Model 747, this picture which includes vehicles and ground equipment gives an appreciation of the true 'jumbo' size of this remarkable transport. The aircraft pictured is the 747-200B *Knut Viking* (SE-DFZ) of Scandinavian Airlines System.

Boeing Model 747SP/747-300 and E-4

China Airlines, based at Taipei, is the flag carrier of the Republic of China (Taiwan). Four Boeing 747SPs ordered by this airline had all been delivered by late 1982 and B-1862 illustrated here was the first to enter service. When all orders outstanding in early 1983 are delivered there will be 40 in use worldwide.

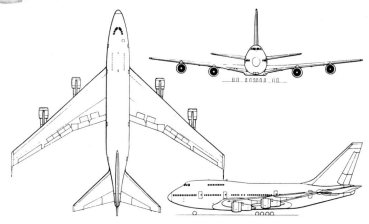

History and Notes

On 3 September 1973 Boeing announced that the company intended to develop a lighter-weight longer-range version of the Model 747 for use on lower-density routes. News came a week later than Pan American had ordered 10 of these aircraft, identified as the Model 747SP (Special Performance).

The Model 747SP is basically similar to the Model 747-100B, the major difference being a reduction of 47 ft 1 in (14.35 m) in overall length. This provides seats for 299 passengers on the main deck and 32 on the upper deck, with a maximum high-density seating capacity of 440. Fuel tankage is also increased. One Model 747SP with 50 passengers established during 23/24 March 1976 a world record for nonstop distance by a commercial aircraft of 10,290 miles (16,560 km), on delivery from Washington to Cape Town.

The Model 747EUD (Extended Upper Deck), in 1982 redesignated Model 747-300, has the upper forward fuselage extended aft by 23 ft 4 in (7.11 m) to increase accommodation in this area from 32 to 69 passengers. This conversion is applicable to all current production versions except the Models 747-200C, -200F and 747SP. Orders for this option are now approaching the 20 mark.

Under the designation E-4 the USAF has acquired four of a planned six Model 747-200Bs equipped as Advanced Airborne Command Post (AABNCP) aircraft, to provide a vital link between the US national command and its retaliatory forces in the event of an attack on the USA.

Specification: Boeing Model 747SP
Origin: USA
Type: long-range commercial transport
Accommodation: flight crew of 3; up to 440 passengers
Powerplant: four 50,000-lb (22680-kg) thrust Pratt & Whitney JT9D-7FW turbofans
Performance: maximum speed 609 mph (980 km/h) at 30,000 ft (9145 m); service ceiling 45,100 ft (13745 m); range with fuel reserves and 331 passengers 6,736 miles (10,841 km)
Weights: empty operating 325,000 lb (147418 kg); maximum take-off 700,000 lb (317515 kg)
Dimensions: span 195 ft 8 in (59.64 m); length 184 ft 9 in (56.31 m); height 65 ft 5 in (19.94 m); wing area 5,500.0 sq ft (510.95 m²)

Boeing 747SP

Right: The long-range Boeing Model 747SP HZ-AIF of Saudi Arabian Airlines, the first of two acquired by the operator for use on non-stop services from Jeddah to New York and the Far East.

Below: Among its all-747 fleet, Qantas Airways of Australia has two of Boeing's longer-range 747SPs. Illustrated is VH-EAA, *City of Gold Coast/Tweed*, the other is VH-EAB *City of Winton*. On 1-3 May 1976 one of Pan American's 747SPs established a round-the-world speed record of 502.8 mph (809.2 km/h).

Boeing Model 757

British Airways and Eastern Airlines were the launching airlines for the new Boeing Model 757, and Eastern had four of their 21 on order in service in early 1983. The aircraft of both operators are powered by Rolls-Royce RB.211 turbofans, making this the first Boeing airliner to be introduced with a non-American engine.

History and Notes

Boeing announced in early 1978 its intention of developing a new advanced-technology short/medium-range commercial transport. Identified as the Model 757, it has a new wing, makes use of the Model 727 fuselage and is powered by two advanced fuel-efficient turbofan engines. Following the finalization of contracts with British Airways and Eastern Air Lines for 19 and 21 aircraft respectively, Boeing announced on 23 March 1979 that production had been initiated. The first of these aircraft (N757A) was rolled out on 13 January 1982 and made its maiden flight on 19 February 1982. The initial production version is the Model 757-200, and first deliveries were made on schedule, Eastern Airlines operating its first revenue flight on 1 January 1983.

To achieve the simultaneous launch of this programme and of the Model 767, Boeing has had to rely on national and international co-operation. For example, the airframe has assemblies/components produced by Avco Aerostructures, Boeing Vertol, Fairchild Republic, Grumman, Heath Tecna and Schweizer in the US, and by CASA in Spain, Hawker de Havilland in Australia and Short Brothers in Northern Ireland. The Rolls-Royce RB.211-535 engines that are powering early production aircraft are expected to show a fuel saving of some 45 per cent per passenger by comparison with the engines of current medium-range aircraft.

Orders and options for some 180 aircraft have been received, the major buyer being Delta Air Lines with 60 on order.

Specification: Boeing Model 757

Origin: USA
Type: short/medium-range commercial transport
Accommodation: flight crew of 2; up to 224 passengers
Powerplant: two 37,400-lb (16964-kg) thrust Rolls-Royce RB.211-535C turbofans
Performance: (estimated with 186 passengers) cruising speed Mach 0.80; maximum range 2,383 miles (3835 km)
Weights: empty operating 130,420 lb (59158 kg); maximum take-off 220,00 lb (99790 kg)
Dimensions: span 124 ft 6 in (37.95 m); length 155 ft 3 in (47.32 m); height 44 ft 6 in (13.56 m); wing area 1,951.0 sq ft (181.25 m²)

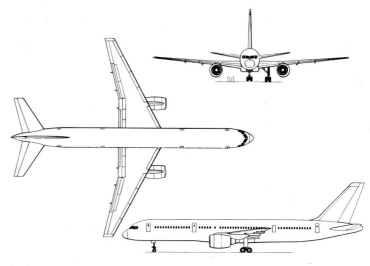

Boeing 757-200

The new generation of Boeing airliners, the Model 757 and 767 were at the beginning of what must surely be a successful career in early 1983. This aircraft in the insignia of Britain's Monarch Airlines, based at Luton, is one of three 757-200s which this operator was to introduce into service during 1983.

British Airways was one of the two launching airlines for Boeing's new Model 757, and shown in this illustration is G-BIKA *Dover Castle*, the first of 17 to enter service with British Airways. Their revenue operations with the type began on 9 February 1982, on the London Heathrow-Belfast Shuttle service.

Boeing Model 767

Boeing's second new-technology turbofan-powered aircraft of the 1980s is the 767, differing from the contemporary 757 by its wider fuselage. This has a cabin with a maximum width of 15 ft 6 in (4.72 m), giving basic seating for 211 passengers: 18 first-class seated six-abreast and 193 tourist class seven-abreast.

History and Notes

Simultaneously with the announcement of its intention to develop the Model 757, Boeing revealed that a wider-body Model 767, to permit a two-aisle seating layout, would be introduced at the same time. Definition of its design benefitted from the participation of United Air Lines, and following receipt of an order for 30 of these aircraft from UAL, Boeing announced on 14 July 1978 the initiation of full-scale development. Construction began a year later and the first (N767BA) was rolled out on 4 August 1981. This flew for the first time on 26 September, and following certification on 30 July 1982 deliveries to UAL began the following month, the airline making an inaugural flight with the type, between Chicago and Denver, on 8 September 1982.

Similar in overall configuration to the Model 757, the Model 767 differs primarily by its 15 ft 6 in (4.72 m) wide cabin and in having a flight deck specifically designed for two-crew operation. Power is provided by advanced-technology fuel-efficient engines, initially Pratt & Whitney JT9D-7R4D turbofans. As in the case of the 757, its production is the result of national/international collaboration, involving Canada, Italy and Japan as well as the USA. The initial production version is designated Model 767-200 and orders and options for more than 300 aircraft have been received. Major operators will include Air Canada, All Nippon, American Airlines, Delta Air Lines, TWA and United Airlines.

Specification: Boeing Model 767
Origin: USA
Type: medium-range commercial transport
Accommodation: flight crew of 2; up to 289 passengers
Powerplant: two 47,800-lb (21682-kg) thrust Pratt & Whitney JT9D-7R4D turbofans
Performance: (provisional) cruising speed Mach 0.80; service ceiling 39,000 ft (11885 m); range 3,200 miles (5150 km)
Weights: empty operating 179,082 lb (81230 kg); maximum take-off 300,000 lb (136078 kg)
Dimensions: span 156 ft 1 in (47.57 m); length 159 ft 2 in (48.51 m); height 52 ft 0 in (15.85 m); wing area 3,050.0 sq ft (283.35 m²)

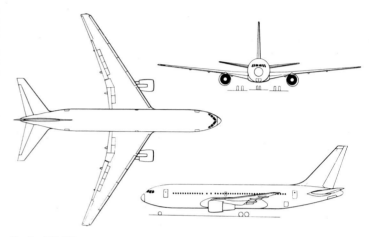

Boeing 767-200

The Model 767 entered service first with United Air Lines which placed the launching order in July 1978. They are powered by Pratt & Whitney JT9D-7R4D turbofan engines, which were expected to give these aircraft a 35 per cent fuel saving over the aircraft they replaced, as well as providing much quieter operation.

The clean exterior of this modern airliner, the Boeing 767, is matched by a superbly furnished interior. It is complemented by advanced avionics including an inertial reference system, air data and flight management computers, flight control system and triplicated digital flight control computers.

Boeing Vertol 234 Commercial Chinook

British Airways Helicopters Model 234LRs have standard fuel tankage and 44-passenger capacity. Two ordered by Arco Alaska for offshore operations will have only 17-passenger capacity, but internal auxiliary fuel tanks will give these helicopters a potential long-range capability of 1,000 miles (1609 km).

History and Notes

In 1956 Boeing Vertol began the development of an all-weather transport helicopter for use by the US Army, and this entered service as the CH-47 Chinook. Its extensive use and the product improvement and refinement that results from some 20 years of military service led the company to announce in 1978 a civil counterpart for commercial use. Two versions were planned and the first to fly, on 19 August 1980, was the long-range Model 234LR which received CAA and FAA certification during June 1981. An initial order for three (increased later to six) aircraft was received from British Airways Helicopters, and this operator introduced the first into service on 1 July 1981: they are used mainly for North Sea oil rig support. Other orders have been received from Arco Alaska, Asahi Helicopter of Japan and Helikopter Service A/S of Norway.

The Model 234LR is identified easily by fairings on each side of the fuselage, twice the size of those on military Chinooks, which house large fuel tanks. Internally the Model 234LR is equipped to airline standards for passenger, passenger/freight or all-cargo use. The utility 234UT has internal fuel tanks, the external fairings being removed. Conversion from LR to UT configuration, or vice versa, can be done in about eight hours.

Specification: Boeing Vertol Model 234LR
Origin: USA
Type: commercial transport helicopter
Accommodation: flight crew of 2; up to 44 passengers
Powerplant: two 4,075-shp (3039-kW) Avco Lycoming AL 5512 turboshafts
Performance: maximum cruising speed 167 mph (269 km/h) at 2,000 ft (610 m); economic cruising speed 155 mph (249 km/h) at 2,000 ft (610 m); operational ceiling 15,000 ft (4570 m); range with fuel reserves and 44 passengers 661 miles (1064 km)
Weights: empty operating 26,403 lb (11976 kg); maximum take-off 48,500 lb (21999 kg)
Dimensions: rotor diameter, each 60 ft 0 in (18.29 m); length, rotors turning 99 ft 0 in (30.18 m); height 18 ft 7¾ in (5.68 m); rotor disc area, total 5,654.9 sq ft (525.34 m²)

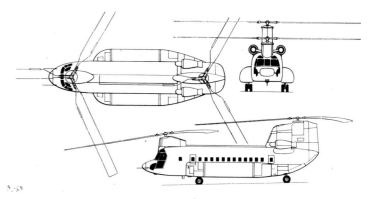

Boeing Vertol 234 Commercial Chinook

This Boeing Vertol Model 234LR Commercial Chinook is based on the military helicopter which has seen such extensive service with the US Army. In the UK British Airways Helicopters has acquired six for use primarily in support of gas and oil exploration/exploitation operations in the North Sea.

Bristol Britannia

A Britannia 253C of Gemini Air Transport, Ghana. The number of Britannias that now remain in airline service can be counted on the fingers of two hands. The Bristol company had once believed that this early turboprop-powered aircraft, often called 'Beautiful Britannia', would win major orders.

History and Notes

In 1947 the Bristol Aircraft Company submitted its Type 175 design to meet a British Overseas Airways Corporation requirement for a civil transport. The Type 175 was a pressurized low-wing monoplane with retractable tricycle landing gear, intended to be powered by four Bristol Centaurus piston engines. Three prototypes were ordered on 5 July 1948, but design revision delayed the first flight (G-ALBO) until 16 August 1952. The initial 90-seat (tourist-class) Britannia Series 100 production version, of which 15 with 3,780-eshp (2819-ekW) Bristol Proteus 705 turboprop engines were built for BOAC, entered service on 1 February 1957. None of these Britannia 100s remains in airline service today.

A Britannia Series 300 with greater capacity and transatlantic range was developed, but BOAC ordered instead a longer-range Series 310, which it introduced on its London-New York service on 19 December 1957. Although it had seemed the Britannia might win large export orders, it could not compete against the new generation of turbojets, and only 60 civil airliners were produced. Short Brothers and Harland built 23 Britannia C.Mk 1s for the RAF's Transport Command and under licence in Canada Canadair produced 33 CL-28 Argus maritime reconnaissance aircraft based on the Britannia, and a number of CL-44 civil/military transports. Only a small number of Britannias, mostly used as freighters, remains in service in 1983.

Specification: Britannia Series 310
Origin: UK
Type: commercial transport
Accommodation: flight crew of 5; up to 133 passengers
Powerplant: four 4,120-eshp (3072-ekW) Bristol Proteus 755 turboprops
Performance: maximum speed 397 mph (639 km/h); cruising speed 357 mph (575 km/h); service ceiling 24,000 ft (7315 m); range with maximum payload 4,268 miles (6869 km)
Weights: empty 82,537 lb (37438 kg); maximum take-off 185,000 lb (83915 kg)
Dimensions: span 142 ft 3 in (43.36 m); length 124 ft 3 in (37.87 m); height 37 ft 6 in (11.43 m); wing area 2,075.0 sq ft (192.77 m²)

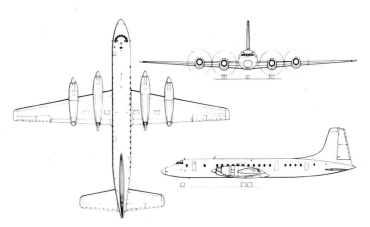

Bristol Britannia 310

Britannia 253C of Redcoat Air Cargo, the airline's only example of the type. British Overseas Airways Corporation was the original customer for the Britannia, introducing it on its routes to South Africa and Australia in February and March 1957. However, a longer-range variant was needed for transatlantic use.

British Aerospace (Avro/HS) 748

The British Aerospace HS 748 twin-turboprop passenger/freight transport now has a reputation for reliability and versatility. Bahamasair, national airline of the Bahamas, has four 748s in its small fleet and these have proved valuable for varied use on this operator's domestic and international services.

History and Notes

Starting as an Avro project in 1958, the Type 748 was designed to provide airlines with a 20-seat feeder transport. However, it failed to gain any interest with this capacity and its design was scaled up, and then in 1959 the Hawker Siddeley Group, of which Avro was a component, decided to build four prototypes, the first (G-APZV) flying on 24 June 1960 and accommodating up to 44 passengers. Power was provided by two Rolls-Royce Dart turboprops, mounted high on the wing leading edge. The HS 748 Series 1 production version was flown first on 31 August 1961; it differed by having 1,740-eshp (1298-ekW) Dart 514 engines and seats for up to 48 passengers.

HS 748 Series 2 748 aircraft with 1,910-eshp (1424-ekW) Dart 531s and 52 seats were followed by HS 748 Series 2A machines with more engine power; they became available also in a Military Transport version and as the HS 748 Coastguarder for maritime patrol. Current production version is the HS 748 Series 2B introduced in 1979, marketed in the USA as the Intercity 748. This has Dart 536-2 engines for improved 'hot-and-high' performance, a slight increase in wing span and other refinements and is available in the same variants as the HS 748 Series 2A. Initial deliveries of a further improved HS 748 Series 2B Super began in 1983, and these introduced a number of refinements. Sales of HS 748s of all series are nearing the 400 mark, in mid-1982, this including 31 supplied to the RAF as Andover C.Mk 1 utility transports.

Specification: BAe HS 748 Series 2B
Origin: UK
Type: passenger/freight transport
Accommodation: flight crew of 2; up to 58 passengers
Powerplant: two 2,280-eshp (1,700-ekW) Rolls-Royce Dart RDa.7 Mk 536-2 turboprops
Performance: cruising speed at weight of 38,000 lb (17237 kg) 281 mph (452 km/h); service ceiling 25,000 ft (7620 m); range with maximum payload and fuel reserves 904 miles (1455 km)
Weights: empty operating 26,910 lb (12206 kg); maximum take-off 46,500 lb (21092 kg)
Dimensions: span 102 ft 5½ in (31.23 m); length 67 ft 0 in (20.42 m); height 24 ft 10 in (7.57 m); wing area 828.87 sq ft (77.00 m²)

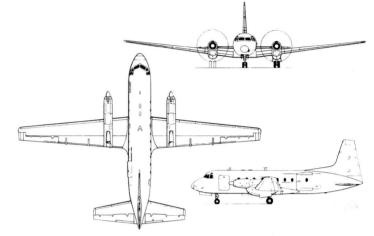

British Aerospace (HS) 748 Series 2A

Philippine Airlines selected HS 748s for similar operations to those of Bahamasair. These two operators are typical of airlines around the world that have kept the production line ticking over for more than 20 years. Steady product improvement has been a key factor, which has now led to the new and advanced 2B Super.

British Aerospace (HP/Scottish Aviation) Jetstream

Apollo Airways of Goleta, California has some 10 British Aerospace Jetstream Is in its 16-aircraft fleet, these providing commuter services in California. Apollo's Jetstreams are being modified under a programme devised by the UK company Aeronautical Development Associates; modified aircraft are known as Apollo Jetstreams.

History and Notes

Handley Page Ltd finalized the design of a twin-turboprop executive/commuter transport designated H.P.137, and a decision to build four prototypes was made in January 1966. However, the company went into liquidation in August 1969 before certification was gained, and although attempts were made to continue production with financial backing from the USA, it was Scottish Aviation that later manufactured the Jetstream. Even this company later lost its identity, becoming the Scottish Division of British Aerospace Aircraft Group on 1 January 1978.

Early success seemed assured by an order from the USAF for a militarized Jetstream 3M (C-10A) but this was later cancelled. Handley Page and its successor built and flew 38 civil Jetstream 200s, Jetstream Aircraft built five and Scottish Aviation another five and most of these were sold in the USA; many were modified later by Riley Aircraft of Carlsbad, California, the improved Riley Jetstream having Astazou XVI engines. Scottish Aviation built the Jetstream 201s used by the RAF and Royal Navy as Jetstream T.Mk 1 and T.Mk 2 respectively, plus a small number of civil aircraft. A new lease of life is promised by the decision to develop a Jetstream 31 with 900-shp (671-kW) Garrett TPE331-10 turboprops, the first production example of which (G-TALL) was flown on 18 March 1982. Contactair of Stuttgart received the first of three on 15 December 1982.

Specification: BAe Jetstream Series 200
Origin: UK
Type: executive/commuter transport
Accommodation: flight crew of 1 or 2; up to 16 passengers
Powerplant: two 996-eshp (743-ekW) Turboméca Astazou XVI C2 turboprop engines
Performance: maximum cruising speed 282 mph (454 km/h) at 10,000 (3050 m); service ceiling 25,000 ft (7620 m); range with maximum fuel and reserves 1,380 miles (2221 km)
Weights: empty 7,683 lb (3485 kg); maximum take-off 12,566 lb (5700 kg)
Dimensions: span 52 ft 0 in (15.85 m); length 47 ft 1½ in (14.36 m); height 17 ft 5½ in (5.32 m); wing area 270.0 sq ft (25.08 m²)

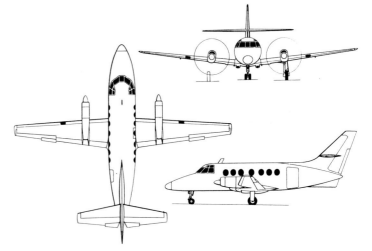

British Aerospace (HP/Scottish) Jetstream 31

G-TALL illustrated is the prototype Jetstream 31, but the first UK operator is Peregrine Air Services of Aberdeen, which received the first of two aircraft on order on 30 December 1982. These have QC (quick change) interiors for rapid conversion from 18-seat commuter to 12-seat executive layout.

British Aerospace (HS) 125

Once dwarfed by the company's Boeing 747s, this true Hawker Siddeley HS 125-3B of Qantas Airways is no longer in operation. It has given valuable service as a pilot trainer and for use in a communications role. Many of these aircraft are operated in North America, primarily in the role of executive business jets.

History and Notes

Development of the British Aerospace HS 125 business transport was started in 1961 by the de Havilland company. The first of two D.H.125 prototypes (G-ARYA) flew on 13 August 1962, powered by 3,000-lb (1361-kg) thrust Bristol Siddeley Viper 20 turbojets. Production D.H.125 Series 1 aircraft followed, with similarly powered Viper 520 engines; later D.H.125 Series 1A/1Bs had Viper 521s and 522s of 3,100-lb (1406-kg) thrust. In mid-1963 de Havilland became part of the Hawker Siddeley group, which continued development of this aircraft as the HS 125.

The HS 125 Series 2 comprised 20 Dominie T.Mk 1 navigation trainers for the RAF, which acquired also CC.Mk 1 and Mk 2 communications HS 125s from later series. HS 125 Series 3 and Series 400 aircraft differed primarily by having more powerful variants of the Viper 522, but the following HS 125 Series 600 introduced a fuselage 'stretch' of 3 ft 1 in (0.94 m) to provide seating for up to 14 passengers. In current production is the HS 125 Series 700 with Garrett TFE731 turbofan engines and many refinements; export versions are designated HS 125 Series 700A (North America) and HS 125 Series 700B (other nations). Also available is the Protector maritime surveillance version equipped with search radar and other specialized equipment. Nearly 200 HS 125 Series 700 aircraft have been ordered worldwide, and of this number about 70 per cent are for customers in North America.

Specification: BAe HS 125 Series 700
Origin: UK
Type: business transport
Accommodation: flight crew of 2; up to 14 passengers
Powerplant: two 3,700-lb (1678-kg) thrust Garrett TFE731-3-1RH turbofans
Performance: maximum cruising speed 502 mph (808 km/h) at 27,500 ft (8380 m); economic cruising speed 449 mph (723 km/h) at 41,000 ft (12495 m); service ceiling 41,000 ft (12495 m); range with fuel reserves and maximum payload 2,785 miles (4482 km)
Weights: empty 12,845 lb (5826 kg); maximum take-off 25,500 lb (11567 kg)
Dimensions: span 47 ft 0 in (14.33 m); length 50 ft 8½ in (15.46 m); height 17 ft 7 in (5.36 m); wing area 353.0 sq ft (32.79 m²)

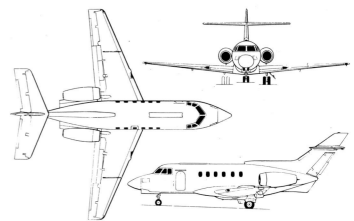

British Aerospace (HS) 125 Series 700

Right: An unusual view of the British Aerospace HS 125 business transport. It shows the porous stainless steel panels on wing and tail unit leading-edges which are part of an effective liquid anti-icing/de-icing system, wing fences inboard of the ailerons to improve lateral stability, and the clean powerplant installation.

Below: Starting life in 1962 as the de Havilland D.H.125, subsequently the Hawker Siddeley HS 125, this popular business transport continues in production in 1983 as the British Aerospace HS 125 Series 700. This was the first to have new fuel-efficient and quieter turbofan engines, available also as retrofits for earlier versions.

British Aerospace (BAC) One-Eleven

The British Aerospace One-Eleven illustrated in this profile is one of the three Series 500s operated by Cyprus Airways in 1983.

History and Notes

The British Aerospace One-Eleven derives from the Hunting Aircraft H.107 project for a 32-seat turbojet-powered transport. In 1960 Hunting was acquired by British Aircraft Corporation, which continued development as the 59-seat BAC.107. This failed to gain interest, leading to the 79-seat BAC.111 (later named One-Eleven). The basic One-Eleven Series 200 prototype (G-ASHG) was flown first on 20 August 1963. It was introduced into service on British United Airways' Gatwick-Genoa route on 9 April 1965.

The One-Eleven Series 200 (56 built) was followed by the One-Eleven Series 300 (9) with increased payload/range capability, and the similar One-Eleven Series 400 (69) modified to US requirements. The prototype of a larger-capacity One-Eleven Series 500 was flown on 30 June 1967, its fuselage lengthened by 13 ft 6 in (4.11 m); a final variant, the One-Eleven Series 475, combined the Series 400 fuselage with Series 500 wings and powerplant: both were available in executive and freighter variants.

One-Eleven sales totalled 230, but licence construction of these aircraft continues in Romania. Two One-Eleven Srs 525/1s and one One-Eleven Srs 487 freighter were supplied to Romania as specimen aircraft during 1981-2, and Romanian production of Rombac 1-11 aircraft has been started. More than 150 of the British-built One-Elevens remain in service, major operators being British Airways, British Caledonian Airways, Philippine Airlines and USAir.

Specification: BAe One-Eleven Srs 500

Origin: UK
Type: short/medium-range transport
Accommodation: flight crew of 2; up to 119 passengers
Powerplant: two 12,550-lb (5693-kg) thrust Rolls-Royce Spey Mk 512 DW turbofans
Performance: maximum cruising speed 541 mph (871 km/h) at 21,000 ft (6400 m); maximum cruising height 35,000 ft (10670 m); range with fuel reserves and full payload 1,694 miles (2726 km)
Weights: empty operating 53,762 lb (24386 kg); maximum take-off 104,500 lb (47400 kg)
Dimensions: span 93 ft 6 in (28.50 m); length 107 ft 0 in (32.61 m); height 24 ft 6 in (7.47 m); wing area 1,031.0 sq ft (95.78 m²)

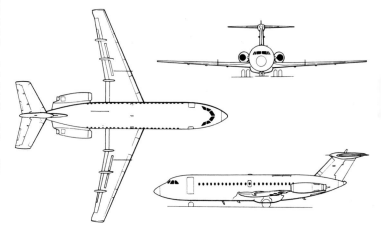

British Aerospace (BAC) One-Eleven Series 475

British Aerospace One-Eleven PI-C1171 in service with Philippine Airlines (now re-registered RP-C1171) is one of 12 One-Eleven Series 500s operated by this company. Despite efforts by British Aerospace to create interest in further-developed variants of this reliable airliner, production has ended in the UK.

UK production of the British Aerospace One-Eleven has ended, but the type will continue to be built for some years in Romania as the Rombac 1-11. The first Romanian-assembled Series 560 (equivalent to Series 500) was flown on 18 September 1982, certificated on 17 December and delivered to TAROM seven days later.

British Aerospace (DH/HS) Trident

British Aerospace Trident 2E (B-250) is in service with CAAC, which is the national carrier of the People's Republic of China. This airline acquired a total of 37 Tridents, their number including Trident 1E, 2E and two Super 3Bs, the latter differing from the standard 3B by having increased fuel capacity.

History and Notes

The Trident originated as the de Havilland D.H.121, to meet a British European Airways requirement of 1956 for a short/medium-range transport. Submissions were made also by Avro and Bristol, but it was de Havilland that gained a contract for 24 D.H.121s on 12 August 1959. The first Trident I (G-ARPA) was flown on 9 January 1962. This had a 'clean' low-set monoplane wing, rear-mounted powerplant comprising three 9,850-lb (4468-kg) thrust Rolls-Royce RB.163/1 Mk 505/5 Spey turbofans, and seats for up to 103 passengers.

When de Havilland merged into the Hawker Siddeley group, the latter company became responsible for development and production of the HS 121 Trident. Later versions were the Trident 1E, with more powerful Speys and seating for a maximum 139 passengers; the further-developed Trident 2E flown on 27 July 1967 and the last major production variant, the Trident 3B. In this version the fuselage was lengthened to seat a maximum 180 passengers and a fourth engine was provided in the form of a 5,250-lb (2381-kg) thrust RB.162-86 turbojet in the aircraft's tail unit, below the rudder. The final variant comprised two Trident Super 3Bs for CAAC, national airline of the People's Republic of China. They differed from Trident 3Bs by having increased fuel and 152 seats. A total of 117 Tridents were built and about 70 remain in service, used by British Airways and CAAC.

Specification: BAe Trident 2E
Origin: UK
Type: short/medium-range transport
Accommodation: flight crew of 3; up to 139 passengers
Powerplant: three 11,960-lb (5425-kg) thrust Rolls-Royce RB.163-25 Mk 512-5W Spey turbofans
Performance: cruising speed 605 mph (974 km/h) at 25,000 ft (7620 m); economic cruising speed 596 mph (959 km/h) at 30,000 ft (9145 m); range with typical payload and fuel reserves 2,464 miles (3965 km)
Weights: empty operating 73,200 lb (33203 kg); maximum take-off 144,000 lb (65317 kg)
Dimensions: span 98 ft 0 in (29.87 m); length 114 ft 9 in (34.98 m); height 27 ft 0 in (8.23 m); wing area 1,456.0 sq ft (135.26 m²)

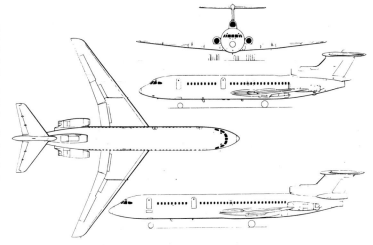

British Aerospace (HS) Trident 2E (lower side view: Trident 3B)

British Aerospace Trident 3B (G-AWZP), in service with British Airways, was designed by de Havilland and developed by Hawker Siddeley. This version introduced auxiliary powerplant in the form of a Rolls-Royce RB.162 turbojet, which serves as a boost engine to improve take-off and climb performance.

British Aerospace (HS) 146

The BAe 146, shown here in the insignia of Air Wisconsin, has been ordered for service with the Royal Air Force. Two BAe 146-100s will supplement the RAF's transport fleet, and will be evaluated for their suitability to re-equip The Queen's Flight; for this role 146s would have increased fuel to provide longer range.

History and Notes

Hawker Siddeley began development of the HS 146 four-turbofan transport in August 1973. Within months economic problems in the UK brought virtual suspension of the programme until 10 July 1978, when it was resumed by British Aerospace. Production is being undertaken in several company factories, as well as by risk-sharing partners that include Avco Aerostructures (USA) and Saab-Scania (Sweden); Short Brothers in Northern Ireland are manufacturing pods for its Avco Lycoming engines.

Two versions are available, the HS 146 Series 100 for operation from short semi-prepared airstrips, with a seating capacity of 71-93, and a longer-fuselage (by 7 ft 10 in/2.39 m) HS 146 Series 200 for operation from paved runways with 82-109 passengers. The first Series 100 prototype (G-SSHH) was flown on 3 September 1981 and the Series 200 on 1 August 1982, with certification anticipated in late 1982 and early 1983 respectively. The basic configuration is of a high-wing cantilever monoplane with a pressurized circular-section fuselage, a T-tail with swept surfaces, retractable tricycle landing gear and power provided by four Avco Lycoming turbofan engines in pylon-mounted underwing pods.

Orders and options for 26 aircraft had been received by early September 1982 from Dan-Air Services in the UK and Air Wisconsin and Pacific Express Airlines in the USA.

Specification: BAe 146 Series 100
Origin: UK
Type: short-range transport
Accommodation: flight crew of 2; up to 93 passengers
Powerplant: four 6,700-lb (3039-kg) thrust Avco Lycoming ALF 502R-3 turbofans
Performance: maximum cruising speed 483 mph (777 km/h) at 26,000 ft (7925 m); economic cruising speed 440 mph (708 km/h) at 30,000 ft (9145 m); range with fuel reserves and maximum payload 518 miles (834 km)
Weights: empty operating 46,700 lb (21183 kg); maximum take-off 80,750 lb (36628 kg)
Dimensions: span 86 ft 5 in (26.34 m); length 85 ft 10 in (26.16 m); height 28 ft 3 in (8.61 m); wing area 832.0 sq ft (77.29 m²)

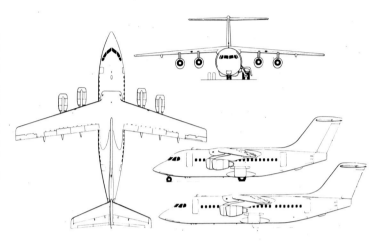

British Aerospace 146 Series 100 (lower side view: Series 200)

The fifth BAe 146-100 completed on 13 December 1982 a seven-week tour of the Far East, Australasia, Malaysia and India during which it carried 3,300 passengers and covered 58,000 miles (93342 km). UK certification by the CAA was gained on 7 February 1983, and Dan-Air inaugurated services with the type at the end of May.

BAe 146 demonstrator G-OBAF. An advantage of the type is the use of four reliable turbofan engines that, in normal operation, are working comfortably below their maximum output. This ensures very low noise levels.

Britten-Norman (Pilatus) BN-2A Mk III Trislander

Trans Jamaican Airlines, based at Montego Bay, Jamaica, operates a mixed fleet of aircraft to provide scheduled passenger services that include routes to adjacent islands. The fleet includes two Islanders and two Trislanders, the excellent range capability of the latter combined with its capacity proving of great advantage.

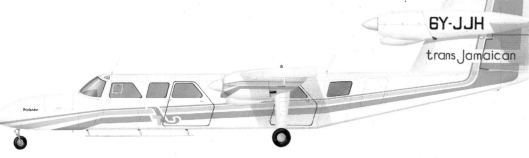

History and Notes

Requests for a 'stretched' Islander to accommodate at least five more passengers could not be satisfied easily. This led to development of a three-engined version of the Islander, dubbed Trislander, with a fuselage lengthened by 7 ft 6 in (2.29 m) to accommodate 17 passengers. The difficult aspect of this conversion from the Islander was to solve the powerplant problem. Weight considerations made a third engine necessary, raising difficulties in ensuring there was no asymmetry of thrust. Sometimes this can be resolved by installing an engine in the nose or at the centre of the wing, but neither solution was acceptable for the Islander configuration. It was decided to incorporate the third engine in the structure of the tail unit, the fin being modified to serve also as an engine mounting.

The prototype Trislander (G-ATWU) was flown first on 11 September 1970 and the first production Trislander was delivered to Aurigny Air Services on 29 June 1971. Production of the Trislander in the UK ended at the beginning of June 1982, following the acquisition of production and worldwide marketing rights by International Aviation Corporation (IAC) of Homestead, Florida. By that time a total of 73 Trislanders had been built and delivered by the UK company, plus 12 kits of components to establish IAC in production. The Trislander is to be marketed in future as the Tri-Commutair.

Specification: Britten-Norman (Pilatus) BN-2A Mk III Trislander
Origin: UK
Type: feederline transport
Accommodation: pilot and up to 17 passengers
Powerplant: three 260-hp (194-kW) Avco Lycoming O-540-E4C5 flat-six piston engines
Performance: maximum speed 180 mph (290 km/h) at sea level; economic cruising speed 150 mph (241 km/h) at 13,000 ft (3960 m); range at economic cruising speed 1,000 miles (1609 km)
Weights: empty equipped 5,843 lb (2650 kg); maximum take-off 10,000 lb (4536 kg)
Dimensions: span 53 ft 0 in (16.15 m); length 49 ft 3 in (15.01 m); height 14 ft 2 in (4.32 m); wing area 337.0 sq ft (31.31 m²)

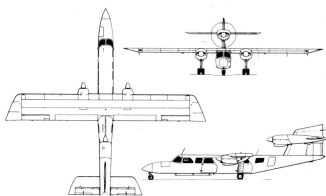

Britten-Norman BN-2A Mk III-2 Trislander

Right: Production of the BN-2A Mk III Trislander by Pilatus Britten-Norman has ended, the manufacturing licence and world-wide marketing rights for this aircraft having been acquired by International Aviation Corporation of Homestead, Florida. Following receipt of FAA certification it was to be marketed as the Tri-Commutair.

Below: The illustration of VP-VAG of St Vincent and Grenadines Air Service, Windward Islands, gives an excellent view of the neat engineering of the Trislander's tail unit to combine aerofoils and powerplant. The adoption of this installation of a third engine provided an economic solution that almost doubled seating capacity of the Islander.

Britten-Norman (Pilatus) BN-2 Islander

Illustrated in this profile is the Britten-Norman BN-2A-8 Islander N35MN *Kiana*, one of a fleet of 10 operated by Munz Northern Airlines in Alaska. They are typical of the usage of the Islander by commuter airlines around the world, its comparatively low initial cost and reliability ensuring continued success.

History and Notes

In 1964 Desmond Norman and John Britten designed a lightweight transport to replace the de Havilland Dragon Rapide and other aircraft of that class. The prototype BN-2 Islander (G-ATCT) flew for the first time on 13 June 1965, then powered by two 210-hp (157-kW) Rolls-Royce/Continental IO-360-B engines. Development brought increased wing span and Avco Lycoming O-540-E engines and this powerplant, in O-540-E4C5 form, is standard in 1983. The first production BN-2 flew on 24 April 1967, entering service some four months later.

The BN-2 was superseded in mid-1969 by the BN-2A, which introduced aerodynamic and equipment improvements, and followed in 1978 by the current production BN-2B with higher landing weight and improved internal design. Optional items introduced over the years include 300-hp (224-kW) Avco Lycoming IO-540-K1B5 engines, Rajay turbochargers for the O-540, wingtip extensions with auxiliary fuel tanks, and an extended baggage nose. It is available also with 400-shp (298-kW) Allison 250-B17C turboprops as the BN-2T Turbine Islander and in Defender and Maritime Defender military versions. Production of all versions, including almost 450 built under licence in Romania and the Philippines, attained the 1,000 mark on 30 April 1982.

Specification: Britten-Norman (Pilatus) BN-2B
Origin: UK
Type: feederline transport
Accommodation: pilot and up to nine passengers
Powerplant: two 260-hp (194-kW) Avco Lycoming O-540-E4C5 flat-six piston engines
Performance: maximum speed 170 mph (274 km/h) at sea level; economic cruising speed 150 mph (241 km/h) at 12,000 ft (3660 m); service ceiling 14,600 ft (4450 m); range with standard fuel 870 miles (1400 km)
Weights: empty equipped 3,612 lb (1638 kg); maximum take-off 6,600 lb (2994 kg)
Dimensions: span, standard 49 ft 0 in (14.94 m); length, standard 35 ft 7¾ in (10.86 m); height 13 ft 8¾ in (4.18 m); wing area, standard 325.0 sq ft (30.19 m²)

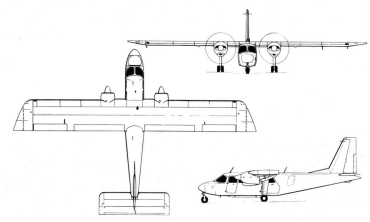

Britten-Norman BN-2B Islander II (dashed lines: wingtips of BN-2A)

The Britten-Norman BN-2 Islander, which came on the market in the second half of the 1960s, was one of the UK's great post-war successes. Financial problems in the 1970s led to a change in ownership of the company, Pilatus Aircraft in Switzerland acquiring all of the assets in September 1979.

Canadair CL-44

Derived from the Bristol Britannia, Canadair's CL-44D had a fuselage stretch of 12 ft 6 in (3.81 m) by comparison with a Series 300 Britannia. It also introduced a swing-tail for freight loading, hinged to swing to starboard at the beginning of the constant section, and was first flown in this form on 16 November 1960.

History and Notes

In March 1954, Canadair Ltd negotiated a manufacturing licence for the Bristol Britannia, the licence covering initially a maritime-reconnaissance version for the Royal Canadian Air Force. Designated CL-28 Argus, the first of these was delivered in the autumn of 1957, differing from the parent aircraft in its unpressurized fuselage and economic turbo-compound piston engines. The RCAF also had a requirement for a freight/troop carrier, and Canadair designed a version of the Britannia with increased wing span and a lengthened fuselage. Designated Canadair CL-44D, 12 were built for the RCAF as the CC-106 Yukon, the last delivered in 1961.

While working on the CL-44D, Canadair's design team thought of an idea to simplify cargo handling: a hinged aft fuselage section to permit straight-in loading or unloading of freight. The resulting CL-44D-4 incorporating this idea became the world's first cargo aircraft to introduce such capability on the production line. By July 1961 The Flying Tiger Line and Seaboard World Airlines had introduced the type into service. Loftleidir acquired three equipped to seat 178 passengers and, later, a still longer CL-44J (Canadair 400) seating 214 passengers. One other variant was the CL-44-O outsize transport, a conversion of a CL-44 by Conroy Aircraft Corporation in the USA, which had developed the Pregnant Guppy and similar transports. Production of civil and military CL-44s totalled 39, and about 13 remain in service.

Specification: Canadair CL-44D-4
Origin: Canada
Type: long-range cargo transport
Accommodation: normally flight crew of 3 or 4 only
Powerplant: four 5,730-hp (4273-kW) Rolls-Royce Tyne 515/10 turboprops
Performance: cruising speed 386 mph (621 km/h) at 20,000 ft (6095 m); range with maximum payload 2,875 miles (4627 km)
Weights: empty 88,950 lb (40347 kg); maximum take-off 210,000 lb (95254 kg)
Dimensions: span 142 ft 3½ in (43.37 m); length 136 ft 10¾ in (41.73 m); height 38 ft 8 in (11.79 m); wing area 2,075.0 sq ft (192.77 m²)

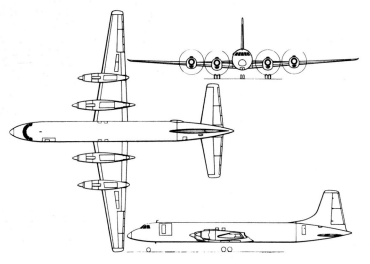

Canadair CL-44D-4

The Flying Tiger Line, known now as Flying Tigers, was one of the first users of the CL-44D. However, it no longer has any in service and now operates a large fleet of modern cargo transports on a world-wide basis. Although close to a quarter-century of service, only small numbers of CL-44s remain in use.

Canadair CL-600 Challenger

The Challenger is available in two versions, which differ primarily by having Avco Lycoming (CL-600) or General Electric turbofan engines. A longer-fuselage CL-610 Challenger E (E = extended) had been planned, to accommodate a maximum of 24 passengers, but for economic reasons its development was abandoned.

History and Notes

Bill Lear, well-known for the family of LearJets, designed the LearStar 600 executive aircraft. When Canadair acquired production rights for this in April 1976 they named it CL-600 Challenger and introduced several changes, the most conspicuous a tailplane shift from low on the fuselage to T-tail configuration.

One feature of its design seemed particularly important to Canadair, a roomy cabin 28 ft 3 in (8.61 m) in length, 8 ft 2 in (2.49 m) wide and 6 ft 1 in (1.85 m) high. Far larger than those of other executive jets, it offered scope for a variety of interior layouts to appeal to a wide spectrum of operators. The Challenger is configured as a low-wing monoplane with swept wings, circular-section pressurized fuselage, T-tail with swept surfaces, retractable tricycle landing gear and rear-mounted engines. Three pre-production Challengers were built, the first flown on 8 November 1978. Canadair carried out a weight- and drag-reduction programme to ensure adequate range, and now offer the aircraft with alternative Avco Lycoming (CL-600) and General Electric CF3401A (CL-601) powerplant, the latter having also drag-reducing winglets. A CL-610 Challenger with lengthened fuselage was planned, but postponed in 1981. Orders total approximately 150, and of this number almost half of them have been delivered.

Specification: Canadair CL-600 Challenger
Origin: Canada
Type: business, cargo and commuter transport
Accommodation: flight crew of 2; up to 19 passengers
Powerplant: two 7,500-lb (3402-kg) thrust Avco Lycoming ALF-502L-2/-3 turbofans
Performance: maximum cruising speed 518 mph (834 km/h); economic cruising speed 463 mph (745 km/h); maximum operating altitude 45,000 ft (13715 m); range with maximum fuel and reserves 3,682 miles (5926 km)
Weights: empty operating 22,825 lb (10353 kg); maximum take-off 40,400 lb (18325 kg)
Dimensions: span 61 ft 10 in (18.85 m); length 68 ft 5 in (20.85 m); height 20 ft 8 in (6.30 m); wing area 450.0 sq ft (41.81 m²)

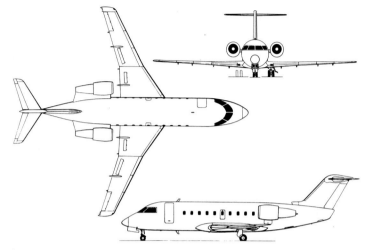

Canadair CL-600 Challenger

Numbered among the new generation of twin-turbofan light business, cargo and commuter transports, the basic design of Canadair's CL-600 Challenger came from the drawing board of the late Bill Lear. It differs from his earlier Learjets by having a cabin that is longer and wider, giving scope for improved layouts.

This near head-on view of Canadair's CL-600 Challenger emphasizes the wide-body fuselage that lifts it out of the single category of an executive business jet. As a result it has a cabin floor area of 202.5 sq ft (18.81 m²) providing ample space for a number of alternative layouts, including a 19-seat commuter.

CASA C-212 Aviocar

Bouraq Indonesia Airlines based at Jakarta is typical of small operators that find aircraft in the class of the CASA C-212 Aviocar to be an invaluable asset. Operating extensive domestic services, they are able to take full advantage of its easy conversion for passenger, cargo or mixed passenger/cargo traffic.

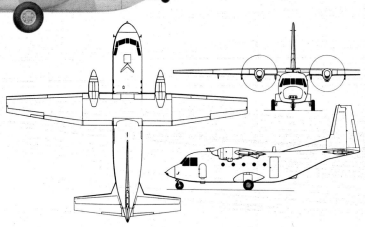

History and Notes

With the Spanish air force operating a variety of transports, including some distinctly vintage specimens, it was decided in the late 1950s to replace them by a standard aircraft. Construcciones Aeronauticas SA (CASA) began design of a STOL transport for the air force in the late 1960s. The first prototype was flown initially on 26 March 1971 and the first C-212A was delivered on 20 May 1974. A cantilever high-wing monoplane with high-lift features for STOL operations, the C-212 has an upswept rear fuselage incorporating a loading ramp/door, a large but conventional tail unit, fixed tricycle landing gear and power-plant comprising two wing-mounted turboprop engines.

From the outset a civil version had been considered, leading to the initial C-212-5 Aviocar series delivered first to Pertamina on 16 July 1975. Powered by 750-shp (559-kW) Garrett TPE331-5-251C turboprops and seating 19 passengers, it remained in production until 1978 when 135 had been built by CASA and 20 by Nurtanio in Indonesia. It was replaced by the C-212 Series 200, the current production versions, of which the first example was flown on 30 April 1978. This differs by having more powerful engines and is certificated for operation at higher gross weight. In addition to the standard utility transport, a C-212 Series 200 ASW and maritime patrol aircraft version is available in 1982, when an ECM/Elint version was under development. Orders for all versions of the Aviocar comfortably exceed 300, of which approximately 240 have been delivered.

Specification: CASA C-212 Series 200 Aviocar
Origin: Spain
Type: STOL utility transport
Accommodation: flight crew of 2; up to 28 passengers
Powerplant: two 900-shp (671-kW) Garrett TPE331-10-501C turboprops
Performance: normal cruising speed 215 mph (346 km/h); service ceiling 28,000 ft (8535 m); range with maximum payload 253 miles (407 km)
Weights: empty 8,333 lb (3780 kg); maximum take-off 16,424 lb (7450 kg)

CASA C-212-200 Aviocar

Dimensions: span 62 ft 4 in (19.00 m); length 49 ft 9 in (15.16 m); height 20 ft 8 in (6.30m); wing area 430.56 sq ft (40.00 m²)

Bursa Hava Yollari was formed in Turkey in 1976 to operate domestic scheduled services. *Sonmez II* (TC-AOC) illustrated is one of two CASA 212-CB Aviocars that formed the initial equipment of this small airline, but these have since been withdrawn from use. The 212-CBs operate at a higher weight than standard 212-Cs.

This shot of the CASA C-212 operated by Korean Air Lines gives a first class impression of the bulk carrying capability of this STOL transport. It has a maximum cargo payload of 6,106 lb (2770 kg), getting on for three tons, but even with this load it is capable of becoming airborne in a run of only 1,445 ft (440 m).

Cessna Model 401/402

TAM, which is the largest third-level airline in Brazil, operates a fleet of aircraft which, apart from three Fokker F.27s, is composed of light twins. Four Cessna 402Bs included in this number find extensive usage on scheduled passenger services which link all major points in Sao Paulo state.

History and Notes

Cessna announced on 1 November 1966 the introduction of two new aircraft: the six/eight-seat Model 401 and the 10-seat Model 402 convertible passenger/freight aircraft. The pair had identical airframes, the configuration being a cantilever low-wing monoplane with conventional tail unit, retractable tricycle landing gear and power provided by two wing-mounted flat-six piston engines. The Model 401 was phased out of production in mid-1972, after 400 had been built, more sales interest being shown in the 10-seat version.

Development of the Model 402 has continued since then, the basic convertible passenger/freight version known since late 1971 as the Model 402 Utililiner. An optional Businessliner version was introduced later, this having an executive style interior for a crew of two and up to six passengers. Mk II versions of both, with factory-installed avionics and equipment (including dual controls), were introduced in late 1975; Mk III versions, with more advanced avionics, appeared in 1978. Cessna have now built something in excess of 1,500 Model 402s, current production centred on the Model 402C.

American Jet Industries developed a turboprop-powered conversion named as Turbo Star. This has two 400-shp (298-kW) Allison 250-B17 engines providing an improvement of almost 27 per cent in cruising speed.

Specification: Cessna Model 402C Utililiner
Origin: USA
Type: convertible passenger/freight transport
Accommodation: pilot and up to nine passengers
Powerplant: two 325-hp (242-kW) Continental TSIO-520-VB flat-six piston engines
Performance: maximum cruising speed 245 mph (394 km/h) at 20,000 ft (6095 m); economic cruising speed 191 mph (307 km/h) at 20,000 ft (6095 m); service ceiling 26,900 ft (8200 m); maximum range with fuel reserves 1,420 miles (2285 km)
Weights: empty 4,106 lb (1862 kg); maximum take-off 6,850 lb (3107 kg)
Dimensions: span 44 ft 1½ in (13.45 m); length 36 ft 4½ in (11.09 m); height 11 ft 5½ in (3.49 m); wing area 225.83 sq ft (20.98 m²)

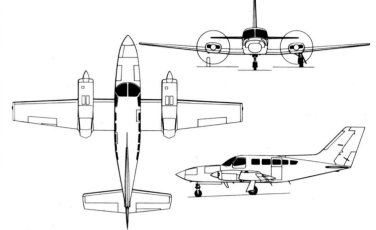

Cessna Model 402C

Cessna's Model 402C is available in 10-seat, cargo, or mixed passenger/cargo layouts under the name Utililiner. There is also an alternative Businessliner, which has an executive interior for a crew of two and up to six passengers. It has proved a popular design for the company with more than 1,500 built.

Cessna Model 404 Titan

Small operators around the world find it valuable to obtain 'off-the-shelf' aircraft in the category of the Cessna Titan. Air Hawaii, based on Honolulu, has no fewer than seven Titans, plus two Model 402s, which it uses to provide scheduled commuter services between the various islands of the Hawaiian group.

History and Notes

Cessna Aircraft Company announced in July 1974 the development of a business/cargo/commuter aircraft to be known as the Model 404 Titan. The model number was dropped subsequently, the aircraft then becoming the Cessna Titan. Similar in overall configuration to the Model 402, the Titan had slightly increased wing span and a longer fuselage providing a cabin 18 ft 9 in (5.72 m) in length, and introduced a tailplane incorporating dihedral. The prototype was first flown on 26 February 1975 and initial deliveries were made in October 1976. Designed specifically for rapid conversion between cargo, commuter and executive passenger roles, the Titan was also able to demonstrate far more economical performance than the Model 402.

As marketed originally, two optional versions of the Titan were available: the Ambassador and Courier. The first was equipped for passenger-carrying, and the second as a utility passenger/cargo aircraft. Subsequently, the Titan Freighter was introduced, with a cargo door as standard and equipped for easy loading and handling of cargo. However, as an economy measure, resulting from the serious recession in the aircraft market in 1982, Cessna announced that production was to be discontinued on a temporary basis. At that time, in early 1982, 378 Titans had been sold.

Specification: Cessna Titan Ambassador
Origin: USA
Type: cargo/commuter/executive transport
Accommodation: flight crew of 1 or 2, and 9 or 8 passengers respectively
Powerplant: two 375-hp (280-kW) Continental GTSIO-520-M flat-six turbocharged piston engines
Performance: maximum cruising speed 250 mph (402 km/h) at 20,000 ft (6095 m); economic cruising speed 188 mph (303 km/h) at 20,000 ft (6095 m); service ceiling 26,000 ft (7925 m); maximum range with fuel reserves 2,119 miles (3410 km)
Weights: empty 4,834 lb (2193 kg); maximum take-off 8,400 lb (3810 kg)
Dimensions: span 46 ft 4 in (14.12 m); length 39 ft 6¼ in (12.04 m); height 13 ft 3 in (4.04 m); wing area 242.0 sq ft (22.48 m²)

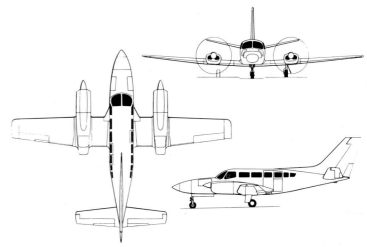

Cessna Model 404 Titan

Very similar to the company's **Model 402**, the Cessna Titan introduced a lengthened fuselage to provide more comfortable accommodation, and the installation of turbocharged engines makes it more economical in operation. This Titan Courier II (G-WTVA) of Executive Express is one of five acquired by this operator.

Cessna Citation I/II/III

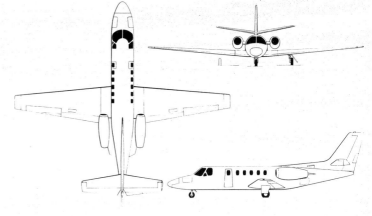

The earlier Citation I, named originally Fanjet 500, is available in standard Citation and, for single-pilot operation, Citation I/SP versions. Combined production of this pressurized seven/nine-seat transport was approaching the 700 mark in early 1983. It has a very high standard of installed equipment.

History and Notes

In late 1968 Cessna announced development of an eight-seat aircraft named Fanjet 500. The name was chosen to reflect the use of turbofan engines to power this new aircraft, a low-wing monoplane with a pressurized fuselage, conventional tail unit, retractable tricycle landing gear and rear-mounted engines. However, after the prototype had flown, on 15 September 1969, the name was changed to Citation.

Modifications made before certification was gained, on 9 September 1971, added a dihedral tailplane, larger vertical tail surfaces and a longer fuselage, and saw the engines mounted farther aft. Citations began to enter service in late 1971, and an improved Citation I was introduced in 1976. This has uprated engines and a wing of increased span; a Citation I/SP is also available, certificated for single-pilot operation. The Citation II, introduced in 1976, has a longer fuselage to seat seven passengers, greater wing span, fuel and baggage capacity, and more powerful engines. A single-pilot operated Citation II/SP is also available. Production of Citation Is and IIs has already exceeded the 1,000 mark. An improved Citation III developed in 1978 has a supercritical swept wing, a longer fuselage to seat up to 10 passengers, a T-tail and more powerful engines. First flown on 30 May 1979 it was certificated on 30 April 1982 and first production deliveries were made towards the end of that year.

Specification: Cessna Citation III

Origin: USA
Type: long-range executive transport
Accommodation: flight crew of two; up to 10 passengers
Powerplant: two 3,650-lb (1656-kg) thrust Garrett TFE731-3B-100S turbofans
Performance: maximum cruising speed 538 mph (866 km/h) at 33,000 ft (10060 m); certificated ceiling 51,000 ft (15545 m); range with fuel reserves and maximum payload 2,671 miles (4299 km)
Weights: empty 10,951 lb (4967 kg); maximum take-off 20,000 lb (9072 kg)
Dimensions: span 53 ft 6 in (16.31 m); length 55 ft 5½ in (16.90 m); height 17 ft 3 in (5.27 m); wing area 312.0 sq ft (28.98 m²)

Cessna Model 550 Citation II

Right: Founder member of a family that now exceeds 1,000 aircraft, the Citation I has since been succeeded by the lengthened-fuselage Citation II and the newly introduced Citation III. This last version has considerably more powerful turbofan engines for operation at a greater gross weight and significantly higher speeds.

Below: Superb setting for a glamorous executive transport, the Cessna Citation II, which is the intermediate member of the Citation range. In a little over 10 years more than 1,000 Citation I/II/III aircraft have been delivered by Cessna, proving the popularity and efficiency of this lightweight turbine-powered transport.

Convair CV-540/-580/-600/-640

Starting life as an air-taxi service to provide a link between Denver and the ski-centre at Aspen, Colorado, Aspen Airways later acquired a fleet of Convair 580s. These were to make it possible for Aspen to gain approval as a scheduled carrier, as well as providing charter services in North America and Mexico.

History and Notes

Early conversions of airliners from piston- to turbine-engine power were not always successful, the aircraft's structure unable to accept the greater output of the turbine engines. No such problem existed with the robust Convairliners, capable of accepting turbine engines without undue airframe stress.

The first conversion was in 1954, D. Napier & Son in the UK installing two of their 3,060-eshp (2282-ekW) Elands in a Convair 340. This flew first on 9 February 1955 and it and five similar aircraft went as Convair 540s to Allegheny Airlines in the USA. Canadair in Canada similarly converted three Convair 440s as Canadair 540s, later building 10 new examples for the RCAF as CC-109s.

In late 1959 PacAero Engineering in the US began conversions of Convair 340/440s with 3,750-shp (2796-kW) Allison 501-D13 turboprops. Known as Convair 580s, or Super Convairs, these seated 52 passengers as the CV-340s had been changed to high-density seating. Convair also ran a programme to install Rolls-Royce Darts in CV-240/-340/-440s. Airframe strengthening and 48-seats optional interior was available on CV-240s, and a 56-seat interior for CV-340/440s. Redesignated CV-240D/-340D/-440D, the first later became Convair 600, the other two Convair 640s. About 240 Convair 580/600/640 conversions were completed, some 140 now remaining in airline service; major operators are Frontier Airlines, Interstate Airlines, Republic Airlines, SMB Stage Lines and Zantop International Airlines.

Specification: Convair 640
Origin: USA
Type: medium-range transport
Accommodation: flight crew of 3 or 4; up to 56 passengers
Powerplant: two 3,025-eshp (2256-ekW) Rolls-Royce RDa.10/1 Dart turboprops
Performance: cruising speed 300 mph (483 km/h); range with maximum payload 1,230 miles (1979 km)
Weights: empty operating 30,275 lb (13733 kg); maximum take-off 57,000 lb (25855 kg)
Dimensions: span 105 ft 4 in (32.11 m); length 81 ft 6 in (24.84 m); height 28 ft 2 in (8.59 m); wing area 920.0 sq ft (85.47 m²)

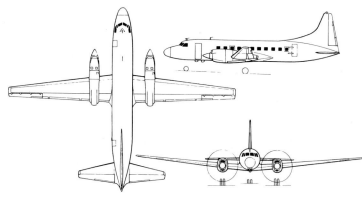

Convair CV-580

Right: This Convair 580 in the latest insignia of Aspen Airways emphasizes the ability of modern exterior decor to give an aircraft a completely new look. Although of an earlier generation of turboprop-powered airliners, the robustly-built Convairs are continuing to provide reliable and economic service for their operators.

Below: Nor Fly Charter A/S of Oslo, Norway, a carrier formed in 1979 to provide passenger and cargo charter operations in Europe, includes in its fleet two Convair 580s. Powered originally by piston engines as Convair 340s, they were the subject of a programme that converted them to turboprop powerplant.

Convair CV-240/-340/-440

History and Notes

Consolidated Vultee Aircraft (Convair) designed in 1945 a Model 110 30-passenger transport for American Airlines, but before the prototype had been flown, on 8 July 1946, the
airlline decided that greater capacity was necessary. Thus was developed the Model 240,
known later as the Convair 240 or Convairliner, which was flown first on 16 March 1947. A
cantilever low-wing monoplane with a slender circular-section fuselage, conventional tail
unit and retractable tricycle landing gear, the CV-240 was powered by two 2,100-hp
(1566-kW) Pratt & Whitney R-2800-S1C3-G radial engines in wing-mounted nacelles.
Convair 240s, seating 40 passengers, entered service on 1 June 1948. In addition to those
built for civil use, a considerable number went to the US Air Force as T-29 trainers and C-131
casualty-evacuation transports.

A developed Convair 340 had more powerful R-2800-CB16/-CB17 engines, greater wing
span and the fuselage lengthened by 4 ft 6 in (1.37 m) to increase seating to 44. The first flew
on 5 October 1951, entering service with United Airlines on 28 March 1952. Further
development of the type led to the Convair 440, flown on 6 October 1955, which introduced
a number of improvements and high-density seating for 52 passengers. Convairliners have
proved robust and reliable, more than 70 of them remaining in service; major operators are
Combs Freightair and Providence Air Charter in the USA.

Specification: Convair 440
Origin: USA
Type: short-range transport
Accommodation: flight crew of 3 or 5; up to 52 passengers
Powerplant: two 2,500-hp (1864-kW) Pratt & Whitney R-2800-CB16 or -CB17 radial piston
engines
Performance: maximum cruising speed 300 mph (483 km/h) at 13,000 ft (3960 m); service
ceiling 24,900 ft (7590 m); range with maximum payload 470 miles (756 km)
Weights: empty operating 33,314 lb (15111 kg); maximum take-off 49,000 lb (22226 kg)
Dimensions: span 105 ft 4 in (32.11 m); length 79 ft 2 in (24.13 m) height 28 ft 2 in
(8.59 m); wing area 920.0 sq ft (85.47 m²)

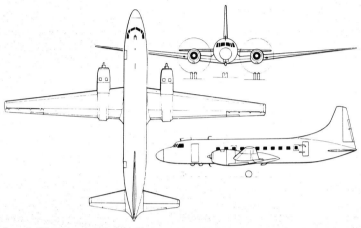

Convair CV-440

Cochise Airlines of Tucson, Arizona, is providing scheduled services within the state
of Arizona, and also serves as a feeder-line operator to major airlines. Convair 440-40
(N136CA) illustrated is one of three 440 Metropolitans that are used, their 52-seat
capacity making them the largest aircraft operated by Cochise.

Convair CV-880/-990

Convair's 880/990 medium-range transports both stemmed from the Convair 600 design, originally named Skylark. First into service was the domestic version, by then redesignated 880 Model 22, and followed later by the improved intercontinental 880 Model 31 which was finally designated 880-M. Production of the two totalled 65.

History and Notes

Convair market research led to design of a civil transport with less capacity but higher performance than the Boeing 707. Construction of a prototype began after the receipt of launching orders for 30 aircraft, and the first aircraft was flown on 27 January 1959 as the Convair 880. Similar in configuration to the Boeing 707, the CV-880 differed primarily by having a more slender fuselage, seating 88-110 passengers.

Known within the company as the Model 32, the CV-880 was intended for domestic services. Only 48 were built for, despite excellent performance and a range of almost 3,000 miles (4828 km), the weakness of the company's research became apparent: its capacity was too small. An improved CV-880-M (Model 31) with intercontinental range failed to sell for the same reason. In attempts to recoup the situation a decision was made to develop a 'stretched' version; but this still retained the narrow-section fuselage. The new Convair 990 (Model 30), with many advanced features and turbofan engines, flew first on 24 January 1961, and entered service with American Airlines and Swissair (which named the type Coronado) in early 1962. However, the shortcomings of hasty design could not be avoided, and all 37 CV-990s that were built had to be modified retrospectively to a new Convair 990A standard, the Convair 880/990 programme proving a costly exercise for the company. Only about a dozen of these aircraft continue in airline service.

Specification: Convair 990A
Origin: USA
Type: medium-range transport
Accommodation: flight crew of 5; up to 121 passengers
Powerplant: four 16,050-lb (7280-kg) thrust General Electric CJ805-23B turbofans
Performance: cruising speed 556 mph (895 km/h) at 35,000 ft (10670 m); service ceiling 41,000 ft (12495 m); range with maximum payload 3,800 miles (6115 km)
Weights: empty operating 120,900 lb (54839 kg); maximum take-off 253,000 lb (114759 kg)
Dimensions: span 120 ft 0 in (36.58 m); length 139 ft 2½ in (42.43 m); height 39 ft 6 in (12.04 m); wing area 2,250.0 sq ft (209.03 m²)

Convair CV-990

To avoid any suggestion that it was of earlier design than the 880, the Convair 600 Model 30 became redesignated Convair 990. Because of design shortcomings it introduced shortened and more streamlined engine pylons and full-span Kreuger leading-edge flaps in an improved version that became designated Convair 990A.

Curtiss C-46 Commando

Rich International's Curtiss C-46F-1-CU Commando illustrated once carried the military serial number 44-78778. It was the last of a batch of 234 C-46Fs and would appear to be the penultimate C-46. It is fairly typical of post-war cargo conversions, the original five-a-side cabin windows having been deleted.

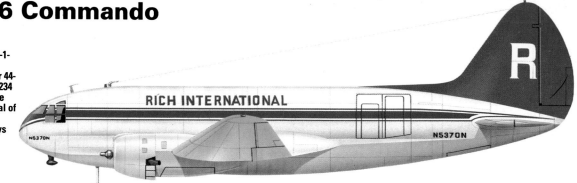

History and Notes

In 1935 Curtiss-Wright began design of a civil transport to compete with the Boeing Model 247 and Douglas DC-3. Identified as the CW-20, the design had a low-set monoplane wing, 'double-bubble' fuselage, twin endplate fins and rudders, retractable tailwheel landing gear and wing-mounted 1,700-hp (1268-kW) Wright R-2600 radial engines. First flown on 26 March 1940, the CW-20 in early testing showed problems solved by a conventional tail unit replacing the twin tail. Known in this form as the CW-20A, the design would almost certainly have entered airline service but for World War II. Instead, it was procured for the US Army Air Force as the C-46 Commando with 2,000-hp (1491-kW) R-2800-43 engines, accommodating 50 troops or 10,000 lb (4536 kg) of cargo; it differed externally by losing most of the 20 cabin windows of the original version. Production of C-46s, and of R5Cs for the US Navy, totalled 3,812.

Large numbers were sold to civil operators post-war, many of them refurbished with airline interiors. Some conversions were quite extensive, including passenger doors with built-in airstairs and reinstatement of all cabin windows, but those for use as freighters differed little from military C-46s. At a peak of deployment, in the early 1960s, C-46s were used by over 90 operators. One of these, Riddle Airlines, evolved a conversion for its fleet of 32 aircraft, designating them C-46R after modification, but now only about 50 of all versions remain in airline service.

Specification: Curtiss C-46R
Origin: USA
Type: medium-range passenger/cargo transport
Accommodation: flight crew of 3 or 4; up to 62 passengers
Powerplant: two 2,100-hp (1566-kW) Pratt & Whitney R-2800-C/CA radial piston engines
Performance: maximum cruising speed 235 mph (378 km/h) at 9,000 ft (2745 m); service ceiling 22,000 ft (6705 m); range with maximum fuel 1,800 miles (2897 km)
Weights: empty 29,300 lb (13290 kg); maximum take-off 50,000 lb (22680 kg)
Dimensions: span 108 ft 1 in (32.94 m); length 76 ft 4 in (23.27 m); height 21 ft 9 in (6.63 m); wing area 1,358.0 sq ft (126.16 m²)

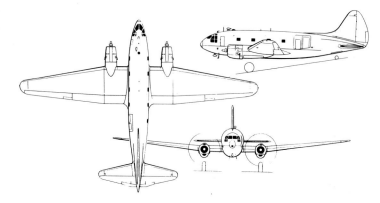

Curtiss C-46 Commando

Air Haiti's HH-AHA *La Perle de Antilles* started life as a Curtiss C-46A Commando military transport. Nearly 4,000 of these aircraft were produced for the US Army Air Force (C-46) and US Navy (R5C), many of them converted post-war for civil use in passenger and cargo roles. Only about 50 were in service in 1983.

Dassault Mercure 100

Market research is important in finalizing aircraft design, but if you don't ask the right questions the answers can be misleading. One can only assume this happened in the case of Dassault's Mercure, for an assumed gap in the market for a 130/150-seat short-haul transport just failed to materialize.

History and Notes

Early sales success of the Mystère/Falcon 20 led Dassault to investigate the market prospects for a short-range airliner in much the same class as the Boeing 737. Sales of the Model 737 confirm the accuracy of Dassault's market research, but the company was able to attract only a single customer for what became known as the Dassault Mercure.

Similar in size and configuration to the Boeing 737, the Mercure has a fuselage 2 in (0.05 m) wider internally, providing seats for a maximum of 162 passengers. Its launch cost was beyond the resources of Dassault, but loan support from the French government amounted to 56 per cent of the estimated initial cost of 1,000 million francs. The company put up 14 per cent of the total, and the balance came from risk-sharing partners that included Aeritalia (Italy), CASA (Spain), F + W (Switzerland) and SABCA (Belgium). Canadair Ltd of Canada was also involved as a sub-contractor. The first prototype (F-WTCC) was flown on 28 May 1971, powered by two 15,000-lb (6804-kg) thrust Pratt & Whitney JT8D-11 engines; the second prototype (F-WTMD) had more powerful JT8D-15 turbofans.

Somewhat imprudently, production began after an order for 10 aircraft was received from Air Inter. This company, which received the first of its fleet on 15 May 1974, was the only customer. The Mercures remain in service, but these are operated with a subsidy from the French government to offset the high cost of spares that results from production ending so rapidly.

Specification: Dassault Mercure 100
Origin: France
Type: short-range transport
Accommodation: flight crew of 2; up to 162 passengers
Powerplant: two 15,500-lb (7031-kg) thrust Pratt & Whitney JT8D-15 turbofans
Performance: economic cruising speed 533 mph (858 km/h) at 30,000 ft (9145 m); range with maximum payload 470 miles (756 m)
Weights: empty operating 70,107 lb (31800 kg); maximum take-off 124,561 lb (56500 kg)
Dimensions: span 100 ft 3 in (30.56 m); length 114 ft 3½ in (34.84 m); height 37 ft 3½ in (11.37 m); wing area 1,248.65 sq ft (116.00 m²)

Dassault Mercure 100

Designed by the very capable Dassault company, benefitting from international collaboration, and incorporating modern technology, the Mercure failed to find the all-essential support from airline operators. Those which are in use by Air Inter have seen almost 10 years of service, but still remain the only order.

de Havilland Canada DHC-3 Otter

In much the same way that Shorts' Skyvan set the pattern for a family of aircraft, de Havilland Canada's DHC-2 Beaver led to the company's highly successful DHC-3 Otter. Although production ended in 1968 considerable numbers remain in service world-wide with operators like Norcanair, used in a variety of roles.

History and Notes

Success with the DHC-2 Beaver light utility transport persuaded de Havilland Canada that there would be a market for a larger-capacity version to seat some 10 passengers, or a cargo load of up to 2,240 lb (1016 kg). This brought development of the STOL DHC-3 Otter, essentially a scaled-up version of the Beaver. Of braced high-wing monoplane configuration, the Otter has fixed tailwheel landing gear and can be operated also with amphibious floats, floats or skis. Power is provided by a Pratt & Whitney radial engine mounted in the nose, despite the belief of some people that operation in the harsh Canadian environment needed twin-engine power. However, de Havilland knew from experience with the Beaver that its Pratt & Whitney powerplant was extremely reliable.

The prototype of the Otter was flown for the first time on 12 December 1951, the initial deliveries being made in 1952. When production ended in 1968 some 460 Beavers had been built, this total including 66 for the RCAF and 227 for the US armed forces, comprising 223 U-1As for the US Army and four UC-1s (later U-18s) for the US Navy. When released by their military operators, many of these Otters found their way on to the civil market and considerable numbers remain in civil use especially with operators in Canada and the United States.

Specification: de Havilland Canada DHC-3 Otter (landplane)
Origin: Canada
Type: STOL utility transport
Accommodation: flight crew of 1 or 2, and 11 or 10 passengers respectively
Powerplant: one 600-hp (447-kW) Pratt & whitney R-1340-S1H1-G or -S3H1-G Twin Wasp radial piston engine
Performance: maximum cruising speed 132 mph (212 km/h); economical cruising speed 121 mph (195 km/h); service ceiling 18,000 ft (5485 m); range with fuel reserves and 2,100-lb (953-kg) payload 875 miles (1408 km)
Weights: empty 4,431 lb (2010 kg); maximum take-off 8,000 lb (3629 kg)

de Havilland Canada DHC-3 Otter

Dimensions: span 58 ft 0 in (17.68 m); length 41 ft 10 in (12.75 m); height 12 ft 6 in (3.84 m); wing area 375.0 sq ft (34.84 m²)

Design features of the DHC-3 Otter included slotted ailerons and trailing-edge flaps, giving good short-field performance, and combination wheel-skis of DH design that allowed in-flight selection of wheels or skis for landing. Otters were used in the US Navy's expedition to the Antarctic during 1956-8.

de Havilland Canada DHC-5E Transporter

Benefitting from development of and experience with the DHC-5 Buffalo, the new DHC-5E Transporter promises its operators excellent performance and reliability. Especially impressive is its STOL capability, able to take off and land in only 950 ft (290 m) and 550 ft (168 m) respectively with a 12,000 lb (5443 lb) payload.

History and Notes

On 9 April 1964, de Havilland Aircraft of Canada flew the prototype of a twin-turboprop STOL utility transport which acquired the designation DHC-5 and the name Buffalo. Like the beast after which it is named, the DHC-5 has proved to be tough and enduring, although built in comparatively small numbers. More than 50 have been sold, and have entered service with the armed forces of Brazil, Cameroun, Canada, Ecuador, Egypt, Kenya, Mauritania, Mexico, Oman, Peru, Sudan, Tanzania, Togo, the United Arab Emirates, Zaire and Zambia.

In June 1979 de Havilland Canada exhibited at the Paris Air Show the demonstration model of a civil counterpart which is designated as the DHC-5E Transporter. The basic structure of the aircraft is virtually the same as that of the Buffalo; it differs by having some system changes and, of course, the military installations are replaced by a civil passenger interior. The cabin also has improved access for passenger operations and is air-conditioned. The standard layout is for 44 passengers in four-abreast seating, but executive and quick-change cargo/passenger interiors are available optionally. Certification for operation at a maximum take-off weight of 41,000 lb (18597 kg) was obtained during 1981, but it is intended to gain certification at a higher take-off weight to allow the Transporter to carry an 18,000-lb (8165-kg) payload.

Specification: de Havilland Canada DHC-5E Transporter
Origin: Canada
Type: general-purpose transport
Accommodation: flight crew of 2; up to 44 passengers
Powerplant: two General Electric CT64-820-4 turboprops, each flat-rated at 3,133 shp (2336 kW)
Performance: maximum cruising speed 287 mph (462 km/h); economic cruising speed 210 mph (338 km/h); service ceiling 31,000 ft (9450 m); range with 14,800 lb (6713 kg) of fuel and payload 115 miles (185 km)
Weights: empty operating 25,200 lb (11431 kg); maximum take-off 41,000 lb (18597 kg)
Dimensions: span 96 ft 0 in (29.26 m); length 79 ft 0 in (24.08 m); height 28 ft 8 in (8.74 m); wing area 945.0 sq ft (87.79 m²)

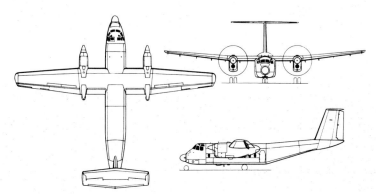

de Havilland Canada DHC-5D Buffalo

Although built in only small numbers, the capability and reliability of the de Havilland Canada DHC-5 Buffalo STOL utility transport is well-known. The DHC-5E Transporter illustrated is a civil version of the current DHC-5D Buffalo, first seen at the Paris Air Show in 1979. It differs mainly in its accommodation and systems.

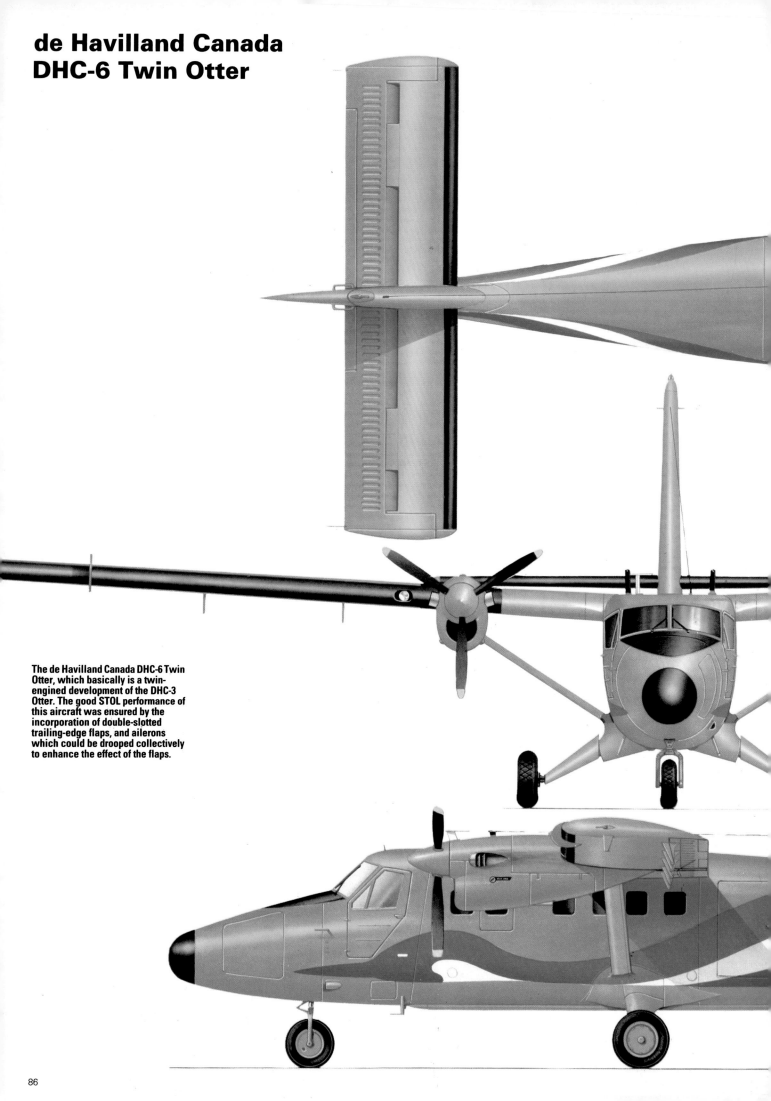

de Havilland Canada DHC-6 Twin Otter

The de Havilland Canada DHC-6 Twin Otter, which basically is a twin-engined development of the DHC-3 Otter. The good STOL performance of this aircraft was ensured by the incorporation of double-slotted trailing-edge flaps, and ailerons which could be drooped collectively to enhance the effect of the flaps.

de Havilland Canada DHC-6 Twin Otter

A significant contribution to the success of the de Havilland Canada Twin Otter was the company's selection of the Pratt & Whitney Aircraft of Canada PT6A engine, which was the first turboprop engine of indigenous manufacture. This combination of high-performance airframe and economic engine has brought world-wide sales.

History and Notes

De Havilland Canada announced in 1964 the development of a turboprop-powered STOL civil transport to seat 13 to 18 passengers. Designated DHC-6 Twin Otter, the first was flown on 20 May 1965. A braced high-wing monoplane with fixed tricycle landing gear, the Twin Otter has a wheeled gear installation as standard, with skis or floats optional, and power provided by two Pratt & Whitney PT6A turboprops in wing-mounted nacelles. The first three aircraft had 579-eshp (432-ekW) PT6A-6s, but Twin Otter Series 100 and Twin Otter Series 200 production aircraft have similarly-rated PT6A-20 engines.

Intended for use by commuter or third-level airlines, Twin Otters serve also with many air forces and government agencies. The first Series 100 aircraft entered service in 1966, followed by the Series 200 which has a lengthened nose and extended rear cabin to provide greater baggage capacity. The current Twin Otter Series 300 has more powerful PT6A-27 engines and a 20-seat commuter interior. Six Twin Otter Series 300S aircraft were developed for an experimental service between STOL airports in Montreal and Ottawa, and available for all versions is equipment for freight carrying and water-bombing. In mid-1982 the company announced the introduction of three Twin Otter Series 300M military versions, each with equipment for a specific role. A total of over 800 Twin Otters has been sold to operators in more than 80 countries.

Specification: de Havilland Canada DHC-6 Twin Otter Series 300 (landplane)
Origin: Canada
Type: utility STOL transport
Accommodation: flight crew of 2; up to 20 passengers
Powerplant: two 652-eshp (486-ekW) Pratt & Whitney Aircraft of Canada PT6A-27 turboprops
Performance: maximum cruising speed 210 mph (338 km/h) at 10,000 ft (3050 m); service ceiling 26,700 ft (8140 m); range with 2,500-lb (1134-kg) payload 806 miles (1297 km)
Weights: empty operating 7,415 lb (3363 kg); maximum take-off 12,500 lb (5670 kg)
Dimensions: span 65 ft 0 in (19.81 m); length 51 ft 9 in (15.77 m); height 19 ft 6 in (5.94 m); wing area 420.0 sq ft (39.02 m²)

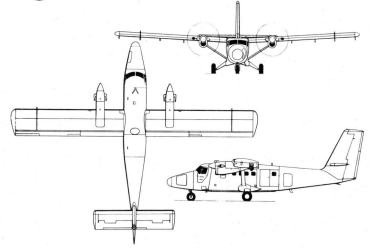

de Havilland Canada DHC-6 Twin Otter Series 300

Golden West Airlines of Newport Beach, California, is described as one of the largest commuter operators in the United States. Much of its success was built up on the reliability of a fleet of DHC-6 Twin Otters, their numbers reducing as they are replaced gradually by de Havilland Canada Dash 7s and, soon, Dash 8s.

de Havilland Canada DHC-7 Dash 7

In 1972, following a wide market survey of short-haul transport requirements, de Havilland Canada began development of the Dash 7 short/medium-range transport. Larger than its immediate predecessors, design emphasis was intended to retain the reliability, short-field performance and economy of the company's earlier designs.

History and Notes

With backing from the Canadian government, de Havilland Canada began in late 1972 the development of a larger capacity short/medium range STOL transport that would provide the higher standards of comfort to be found in much larger airliners. Designated DHC-7, and later named Dash 7, the first of two pre-production aircraft (C-GNBX-X) made its maiden flight on 27 March 1975. The first production aircraft (C-GQIW) was flown on 30 May 1977 and about 80 are already in service, Air Wisconsin and Ransome Airlines then being the major users.

In configuration the DHC-7 is a cantilever high-wing monoplane with a circular-section pressurized fuselage, T-tail, retractable tricycle landing gear with twin wheels on each unit, and power provided by four Pratt & Whitney PT6A-50 turboprops. Access to the cabin, which seats 50 passengers, is via a single airstair door at the rear of the cabin on the port side. There are provisions for optional mixed passenger/cargo or all-cargo operations, and a large freight door can be installed at the forward end of the cabin on the port side. The all-cargo version of the Dash 7 is designated Series 101, and examples serve with the Canadian Armed Forces under the designation CC-132. Orders and options for the Dash 7, received from more than 20 airlines and the Venezuelan navy, have reached a total in excess of 130.

Specification: de Havilland Canada DHC-7 Dash 7
Origin: Canada
Type: short/medium-range STOL transport
Accommodation: flight crew of 2; up to 50 passengers
Powerplant: four 1,120-shp (835-kW) Pratt & Whitney Aircraft of Canada PT6A-50 turboprops
Performance: maximum cruising speed at weight of 41,000 lb (18597 kg) 261 mph (420 km/h) at 8,000 ft (2440 m); service ceiling 21,000 ft (6400 m); range with 50 passengers and fuel reserves 795 miles (1279 km)
Weights: empty operating 27,650 lb (12542 kg); maximum take-off 44,000 lb (19958 kg)
Dimensions: span 93 ft 0 in (28.35 m); length 80 ft 7¾ in (24.58 m); height 26 ft 2 in (7.98 m); wing area 860.0 sq ft (79.89 m²)

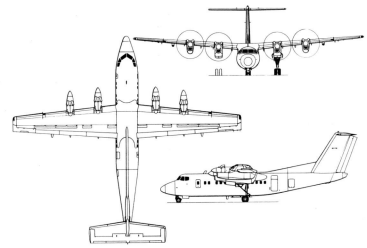

de Havilland Canada DHC-7 Dash-7

Tyrolean Airways of Innsbruck, Austria, numbers two DHC-7 Dash 7s among its mixed fleet of fixed- and rotary-wing aircraft. OE-HLS *Stadt Innsbruck* was the first to be received and, together with OE-HLT *Stadt Wien*, these 50-passenger transports are used to operate the airline's scheduled passenger services.

This illustration of one of three Dash 7s used for scheduled passenger services by Time Air of Lethbridge, Alberta, gives an excellent view of the neat installation of the four PT6A turboprops and of the large tail surfaces. The wings incorporate wide-span double-slotted trailing-edge flaps and upper surface spoilers.

de Havilland Canada DHC-8 Dash-8

The first British customer for the Dash 8 is Brymon Airways, based at Plymouth and Aberdeen. They already operate two Twin Otters and three Dash 7s on provincial services, flying into Heathrow on commuter flights. Brymon plans to open an airport in London's docklands to speed business travel to the City.

History and Notes

To meet growing demands for a quiet short-range transport in the 30/40-seat class, de Havilland Aircraft of Canada initiated the development of such an aircraft under the designation DHC-8 and name Dash 8. It fits in between the company's 19-seat Twin Otter and 50-seat Dash 7 to make a family of aircraft covering a useful range of requirements for commuter and third-line operators. While slightly smaller, the DHC-8 has an overall configuration is similar to that of the Dash 7, being a high-wing monoplane with retractable tricycle landing gear and a T-tail. Power, however, is provided by only two engines, these being advanced-technology turboprops driving large-diameter slow-turning propellers to ensure very low noise levels. Each rated at 1,800 shp (1342 kW), the engines have automatic performance reserve so that, in the event of one engine failing, the other will automatically deliver an output of 2,000 shp (1491 kW).

The Dash 8 will be available in two versions, Commuter and Corporate. The first is the basic aircraft with accommodation for 32 passengers; the second, which will be marketed in North America exclusively by Innotech Aviation of Montreal, will have increased range capability, an auxiliary power unit as standard and will seat, typically, 16 to 24 passengers. Well over 100 orders and options for the Dash 8 have been received by de Havilland Canada, 60 per cent of them from customers in the USA, and the first aircraft was scheduled to make its maiden flight in June 1983.

Specification: de Havilland Canada DHC-8 Dash 8
Origin: Canada
Type: short-range transport
Accommodation: flight crew of 2; up to 36 passengers
Powerplant: two 1,800-shp (1342-kW) Pratt & Whitney Aircraft of Canada PW120 turboprops
Performance: (estimated) maximum cruising speed 310 mph (499 km/h) at 15,000 ft (4570 m); normal range with fuel reserves 656 miles (1056 km)
Weights: maximum take-off 30,500 lb (13835 kg)
Dimensions: span 84 ft 0 in (25.60 m); length 73 ft 0 in (22.25 m); height 25 ft 0 in (7.62 m); wing area 585.0 sq ft (54.35 m²)

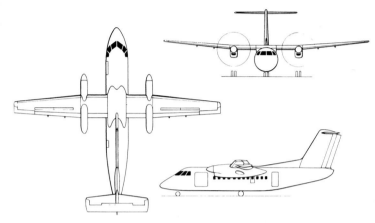

de Havilland Canada DHC-8 Dash 8

An artist's impression of the de Havilland Canada DHC-8 Dash 8 quiet short-range transport shows that it retains the same general lines as its predecessors. The emphasis of its design has been to gain new standards of fuel efficiency and to ensure that it will more than meet new requirements for quiet operation.

Dornier Do 228

AS Norving of Kirkenes, Norway, was the first operator to receive Dornier's new Do 228 twin-turboprop light transport. The version acquired by Norving is the 228-100, which is the basic version with seating for 15 passengers, but it is suitable also for use in freight or mixed cargo/passenger services.

History and Notes

In mid-1975 Dornier began development of an advanced-technology wing (Tragflügel Neuer Technologie, TNT), the prototype structure mounted on a specially modified Dornier Do 28 test-bed aircraft (D-IFNT), which was flown first on 14 June 1979. Successful testing of the wing resulted in its use for the new commuter/utility Dornier 228. On this aircraft the TNT is mounted in high-wing configuration on a fuselage which is similar in cross-section to that of the Do 28/128. The tail unit is conventional, the landing gear of retractable tricycle type, and power provided by two Garrett TPE 331 turboprop engines in wing-mounted nacelles.

The Dornier 228-100 is the basic version, accommodating 15 passengers, and is suitable for deployment in a varity of roles. The first Do 228-100 made its maiden flight on 28 March 1981, and after gaining certification on 18 December 1981 the initial delivery, to AS Norving of Norway, was made in February 1982. The Dornier 228-200 is generally similar, but has a fuselage lengthened by 5 ft (1.52 m) to provide seating for 19 passengers and greater baggage capacity. The first was flown on 9 May 1981 and following certification on 8 September 1982 initial production deliveries were made later in the year. Dornier has received orders and options for both versions which total approximately 100 aircraft, all of them to be completed in commuter configurations.

Specification: Dornier 228-100
Origin: West Germany
Type: commuter/utility transport
Accommodation: flight crew of 2; up to 15 passengers
Powerplant: two 715-shp (533-kW) Garrett TPE 331-5 turboprops
Performance: maximum cruising speed 268 mph (432 km/h) at 10,000 ft (3050 m); economic cruising speed 206 mph (332 km/h) at 10,000 ft (3050 m); service ceiling 29,595 ft (9,020 m); range with 15 passengers and no reserve fuel 1,224 miles (1970 km)
Weights: empty 6,261 lb (2840 kg); maximum take-off 12,566 lb (5700 kg)
Dimensions: span 55 ft 8 in (16.97 m); length 49 ft 4 in (15.04 m); height 15 ft 11¼ in (4.86 m); wing area 344.46 sq ft (32.00 m²)

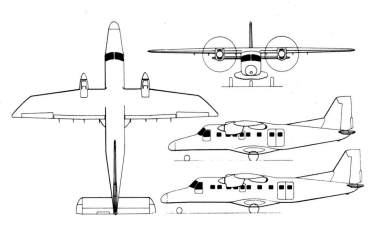

Dornier Do 228-100 (lower side view: Do 228-200)

An advanced feature of the Do 228 is its advanced technology wing which was developed by Dornier with support from the German Federal Ministry of Research and Technology. The wing leading-edge, its raked wingtips, the Fowler single-slotted trailing-edge flaps and the ailerons are all of composite construction.

Douglas DC-3

SMB Stage Lines, which was established in Iowa during 1930, some five years before the Douglas DC-3 was flown for the first time, still numbers three DC-3s in its fleet. However, N41447 is no longer in service, but the profile serves to show the colourful and apt insignia of this commuter airline.

History and Notes

In 1934 Douglas Aircraft began development of an enlarged version of its DC-2 transport to provide a 'sleeper' for use on US transcontinental routes. The resulting DST was flown in December 1935, but it was the DC-3 day version that became a part of aviation history.

By the time of US involvement in World War II, the DC-3 had gained a dominant position in the nation's airlines. The type's capacity and reliability appealed to military planners, and by the end of the war nearly 11,000 had been built in the USA. Licence-construction added about 2,000 in Russia and 485 in Japan. Most of the US-built aircraft served with the USAAF as C-47s or with the US Navy as R4Ds; others went to the nation's allies. When, after the war, these aircraft came on the market many were used without change, but most were modified to bring them to airline standard. Post-war, Douglas developed a DC-3S, or Super DC-3, a lengthened-fuselage 30-seater; prototypes had good performance, but could not compete against more advanced aircraft then entering service. Several companies have since produced re-engined conversions, without conspicuous success. The latest comes from United States Aircraft Corporation of Van Nuys, California, its DC-3 Turbo Express (N300TX) with turboprop engines being first flown on 28 July 1982.

About 450 standard DC-3s/C-47s remain in service with world airlines.

Specification: typical ex-military C-47

Origin: USA
Type: short/medium-range transport
Accommodation: flight crew of 2 or 3; up to 28 passengers
Powerplant: two 1,200-hp (895-kW) Pratt & Whitney R-1830-S1C3G Twin Wasp radial piston engines
Performance: maximum speed 230 mph (370 km/h) at 8,500 ft (2590 m); cruising speed 207 mph (333 km/h); service ceiling 23,200 ft (7070 m); range with maximum fuel 2,125 miles (3420 km)
Weights: empty 16,865 lb (7650 kg); maximum take-off 25,200 lb (11431 kg)
Dimensions: span 95 ft 0 in (28.96 m); length 64 ft 5½ in (19.65 m); height 16 ft 11½ in (5.17 m); wing area 987.0 sq ft (91.69 m²)

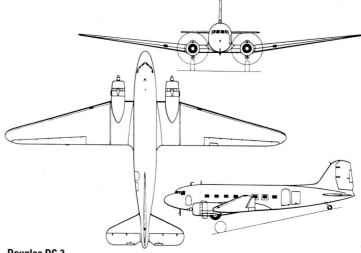

Douglas DC-3

The ubiquitous Douglas DC-3, first flown on 17 December 1935, is also entitled to receive the qualification enduring. In 1983 approximately 450 remained in service worldwide, and it would seem there is little doubt that the type will survive in airline use to be able to claim a remarkable half-century of service.

Douglas DC-4/Canadair DC-4M series

Robust construction and piston-engined reliability have kept DC-4s in use for four decades, but in 1983 only some 35 remained in airline service. Roughly a third were operating in Africa, the remainder in North and South America. Many DC-4s played an important role in the Berlin Airlift of 1948-9.

History and Notes

Before the DC-3 had flown, United Air Lines (UAL) and Douglas began discussing a more advanced airliner of greater capacity. This led to the DC-4 (later DC-4E, E for experimental), an impressive aircraft for its era, seating 42 passengers in a pressurized cabin and introducing many advanced ideas. First flown on 7 June 1938, the DC-4E proved disappointing in tests, and its development was abandoned. Instead, a more simple and lighter-weight DC-4 was put into production, but entry of the USA into World War II meant that these went to the USAAF as C-54 Skymasters, more than 1,000 being built for the armed forces.

When military production ended, Douglas built 79 civil DC-4s and these, plus ex-military C-54s, gave valuable post-war service, particularly during the Berlin Airlift of 1948-9. Variants included 24 aircraft with 1,725-hp (1286-kW) Rolls-Royce Merlin engines developed by Canadair for the RCAF and named North Star. Canadair also built 42 DC-4-M2s with a pressurized fuselage and Merlin engines, 20 for Trans-Canada Air Lines and 22 for British Overseas Airways Corporation, which called them Argonauts. Final variant, the Carvair, was evolved in the UK by Aviation Traders. With a lengthened forward fuselage and a swing-nose they were used for the Channel Air Bridge car ferry, each with five cars and 23 passengers. About 40 DC-4/C-54s remain in service.

Specification: Douglas DC-4
Origin: USA
Type: long-range transport
Accommodation: flight crew of 4; up to 44 passengers
Powerplant: two 1,450-shp (1081-kW) Pratt & Whitney R-2000-2SD1-G Twin Wasp radial piston engines
Performance: maximum speed 280 mph (451 km/h); cruising speed 227 mph (365 km/h); service ceiling 22,300 ft (6795 m); range with 11,440-lb (5189-kg) payload 2,500 miles (4023 km)
Weights: empty 43,300 lb (19641 kg); maximum take-off 73,000 lb (33112 kg)
Dimensions: span 117 ft 6 in (35.81 m); length 93 ft 10 in (28.60 m); height 27 ft 6 in (8.38 m); wing area 1,460.0 sq ft (135.63 m²)

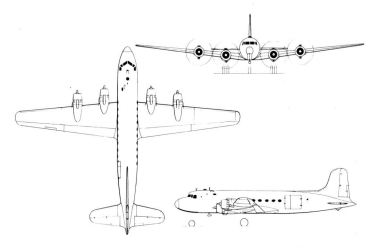

Douglas DC-4

Developed by Douglas when its earlier design for a new passenger-carrier for United Air Lines had proved too advanced, the resulting more basic DC-4 of 1939 served first with the USAAF as the C-54 Skymaster. Built in small numbers post-war, DC-4s and ex-C-54s have proved valuable passenger/cargo carriers.

Douglas DC-6

Although design of the Douglas DC-6 was initiated to produce a military transport for the USAAF, it did not fly until after World War II had ended and is best known as a civil transport. Ordered first by American Airlines and United Air Lines, it entered US domestic service in April 1947 and with European operators in July.

History and Notes

The wartime need of the USAAF for a larger-capacity transport than the DC-4 led to the XC-112A, first flown on 15 February 1946. Too late for use in World War II, it was built to serve post-war airlines as the DC-6, and was used later by the USAF as the C-118A. By comparison with the DC-4 it retained the same wing, but had a lengthened and pressurized fuselage to seat 48 to 52 passengers; an optional high-density layout provided 86 seats. The DC-6 was powered by four 2,100-hp (1566-kW) Pratt & Whitney R-2800-CA15 Double Wasp engines, and the first of 50 for American Airlines was flown on 29 June 1946, entering service on the airline's New York-Chicago route in April 1947.

In 1948 development began of a larger-capacity version, the fuselage being lengthened by 5 ft 0 in (1.52 m) and powered by 2,400-hp (1790-kW) Double Wasp engines. First produced was the all-cargo DC-6A, followed by a similar DC-6B civil transport with seating for 54 passengers but offered later in a 102-seat high-density layout. Last of the civil versions was the convertible cargo/passenger DC-6C, with the special cargo-configured fuselage of the DC-6A provided with cabin windows. DC-6B variants included two with swing-tails modified by Sabena, and a number used for fire-fighting with an underfuselage tank carrying fire-retardant chemicals. Construction of DC-6 and military XC-112A/C-118A and US Navy R6D1s totalled 704, of which about 100 remain in service.

Specification: Douglas DC-6B
Origin: USA
Type: long-range transport
Accommodation: flight crew of 4; up to 102 passengers
Powerplant: four 2,500-hp (1864-kW) Pratt & Whitney R-2800-CB17 Double Wasp radial piston engines
Performance: cruising speed 315 mph (507 km/h); service ceiling 25,000 ft (7620 m); range with maximum payload 3,005 miles (4836 km)
Weights: empty 55,357 lb (25110 kg); maximum take-off 107,000 lb (48534 kg)
Dimensions: span 117 ft 6 in (35.81 m); length 105 ft 7 in (32.18 m); height 28 ft 8 in (8.74 m); wing area 1,463.0 sq ft (135.91 m²)

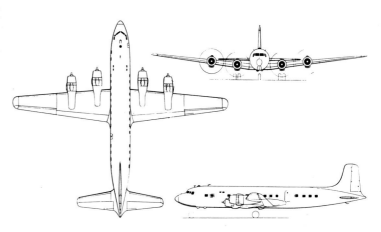

Douglas DC-6

The majority of about 100 DC-6s that now remain in use are being operated in cargo configurations. Many of them are DC-6As, which are 5 ft (1.52 m) longer than the initial DC-6, and incorporate cargo-loading doors and strengthened flooring, but most of the remaining DC-6B/Cs were also converted as cargo transports.

Douglas DC-8

The Douglas DC-8 was the company's first turbojet-powered civil transport to be designed, entering service initially with Delta and United Air Lines in the US. The turbojet powerplant was replaced in later versions by more efficient turbofans and late production Series 50 aircraft had accommodation for up to 189 passengers.

History and Notes

On 7 June 1955 Douglas Aircraft announced its intention of developing a turbojet-powered airliner to supersede the DC-7. A prototype/demonstrator DC-8 was built and when this flew, on 30 May 1958, it was seen to be similar to the Boeing 707. From the outset it was planned to make the DC-8 appeal to a wide range of operators, the type being available with seating capacities from 118 to 176 and with a variety of powerplants. Following certification, on 31 August 1959, the first services were inaugurated simultaneously by Delta Air Lines and United Airlines on 18 September 1959.

Early examples with 13,000-lb (5897-kg) thrust Pratt & Whitney JT3C-6 turbojets were designated DC-8 Series 10, the basic domestic version. The Series 20, also for domestic use, differed only by having 15,800-lb (7167-kg) thrust JT4A-3 turbojets. The Series 30, the first intended specifically for intercontinental use, retained the same airframe but had more powerful JT4A-9 engines; the Series 40, also an intercontinental version, had 17,500-lb (7398-kg) thrust Rolls-Royce Conway 509 turbofans. Finally came the Series 50 with Pratt & Whitney turbofans and with a revised interior layout to seat a maximum 189 passengers. Other specialist requirements were met by manufacture of convertible passenger/freight Series 50CFs and all-freight Series 50Fs. Production of these first DC-8s totalled 294, and about 75 Series 10 to 50 aircraft remain in service.

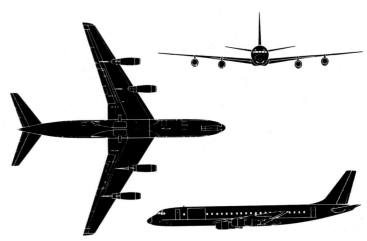

Specification: Douglas DC-8 Series 50
Origin: USA
Type: long-range transport
Accommodation: flight crew of 3 to 5; up to 189 passengers
Powerplant: four 18,000-lb (8165-kg) thrust Pratt & Whitney JT3D-3 turbofans
Performance: maximum cruising speed 579 mph (932 km/h) at 30,000 ft (9145 m); range with maximum payload 5,720 miles (9205 km)
Weights: empty operating 132,325 lb (60022 kg); maximum take-off 325,000 lb (147418 kg)
Dimensions: span 142 ft 5 in (43.41 m); length 150 ft 6 in (45.87 m); height 43 ft 4 in (13.21 m); wing area 2,883.0 sq ft (267.83 m²)

Douglas DC-8-50CF

In 1961 Douglas introduced the DC-8F Jet Trader, a combination cargo/passenger transport, available also in all-cargo configuration without cabin windows. Basic version was the Model 54, derived from the DC-8-50 and with JT3D-3 turbofans. It was followed by the DC-8F-55 with JT3D-3B engines and operating at higher weights.

Douglas DC-8 Super Sixty series

CP Air retains in service a small number of Douglas DC-8 Super 63s, these combining the long fuselage of the Super 61 with the increased wing span and powerplant improvements of the Super 62. The engine pylons were revised to reduce drag and the engine pods redesigned to reduce drag and augment engine thrust.

History and Notes

When Douglas began development of the DC-8, it was intended that it should offer wide flexibility in operation, accounting for the five versions produced. However, this outlook was nowhere near as broad as that of Boeing in marketing the Model 707. Fortunately, the basic design of the DC-8 had potential for growth versions and on 5 April 1965 Douglas announced the intention to develop larger-capacity improved variants of the DC-8 under the Super Sixty (Series 60) designation.

First of these was the Super 61, a lengthened-fuselage version of the late-production Series 50 which has a 'stretch' of 36 ft 8 in (11.18 m) to seat a maximum of 259 passengers on domestic routes. The 189-seat Super 62 was developed for extra long-range services, involving increased wing span, a 6 ft 8 in 92.03 m) fuselage 'stretch', greater fuel capacity and some refinements. Last of these DC-8s was the Super 63, combining the fuselage of the Super 61 with the improvements of the Super 62. As with the original DC-8s, they were available in all-cargo (AF) and convertible (CF) variants, some with structural strengthening for operation at higher gross weights. Six Series 63PFs were also built to Series 63 standard with the structural strengthening of the AF/CF variants. Production of Super Sixties totalled 262 and of these about 200 remain in service.

Specification: Douglas DC-8 Super 63
Origin: USA
Type: long-range transport
Accommodation: flight crew of 3; up to 259 passengers
Powerplant: four 19,000-lb (8618-kg) thrust Pratt & Whitney JT3D-7 turbofans
Performance: maximum cruising speed 600 mph (966 km/h) at 30,000 ft (9145 m); economic cruising speed 523 mph (842 km/h); range with maximum payload 4,500 miles (7242 km)
Weights: empty operating 153,749 lb (69739 kg); maximum take-off 350,000 lb (158757 kg)
Dimensions: span 148 ft 5 in (45.24 m); length 187 ft 5 in (57.12 m); height 42 ft 5 in (12.93 m); wing area 2,927.0 sq ft (271.92 m²)

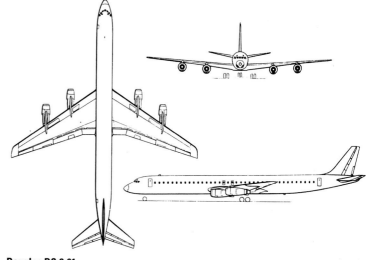

Douglas DC-8-61

DC-8 Super 63s now represent the largest proportion of Super Sixty versions that remain in airline use world-wide. Most of these are in DC-8F convertible cargo/passenger configurations, which allows considerable flexibility in operation, but Super Sixty conversions now number some two-thirds of all in-use DC-8s.

Douglas DC-8 freighter conversions/DC-8 Super Seventy series

Overseas National Airways based at John F. Kennedy International Airport, New York has an unusual function as a leasing carrier. This means that it operates no routes on its own behalf but, instead, has a fleet of aircraft that are in use to provide additional capacity for other airlines. Most of its fleet are DC-8s.

History and Notes

In early 1976 Douglas Aircraft Company launched a programme to modify DC-8 passenger aircraft into specialized freighters. This involves the removal of all passenger equipment, and the installation of a freighter seven-track floor. Other work introduces a main-deck cargo door measuring 85 x 140 in (2.16 x 3.56 m), replacement of the cabin windows by metal plugs, and the provision of a cargo loading system. This remains a current programme in 1983.

In 1979, Douglas announced details of a plan to upgrade DC-8 Series 61, 62 and 63 aircraft by the installation of advanced-technology turbofans, the resulting conversions being designated Series 71, 72 and 73 respectively. Chosen powerplant is the General Electric/SNECMA CFM56, with the Pratt & Whitney JT8D-209 optional.

This programme is managed by Cammacorp of Los Angeles, California and in addition to engine conversion an optional auxiliary power unit and environmental control system can be installed. The first modification of a DC-8 Series 61 was completed in 1981, the resulting Super 71 making its first flight on 15 August. Since then the company has received about 130 orders and options for conversions. Douglas claim these to be the quietest large four-engined transports in service, offering a true noise reduction of some 70 per cent without any loss of performance.

Specification: Douglas DC-8 Super 72
Origin: USA
Type: extra long-range transport
Accommodation: flight crew of 3; up to 189 passengers
Powerplant: four 24,000-lb (10886-kg) thrust General Electric/SNECMA CFM56 turbofans
Performance: (estimated) maximum speed 600 mph (966 km/h); cruising speed 531 mph (855 km/h) at 35,000 ft (10670 m); range with maximum payload 7,220 miles (11619 km)
Weights: empty operating 152,600 lb (69218 kg); maximum take-off 335,000 lb (151953 kg)
Dimensions: span 148 ft 5 in (45.24 m); length 157 ft 5 in (47.98 m); height 42 ft 5 in (12.93 m); wing area 2,927.0 sq ft (271.92 m²)

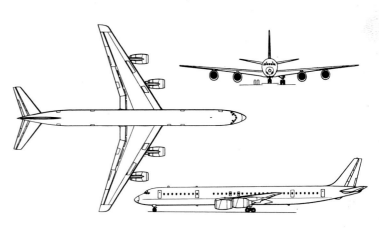

Douglas DC-8-71

With the first Super Seventy conversion gaining certification in April 1982, comparatively few of these improved versions of the DC-8 are yet in service. Although the company has highlighted the considerable noise reduction offered by the CFM56 engines, they are shown to give improved performance and significant fuel savings.

Douglas DC-9

EC-BIN, a Douglas DC-9-32, is one of the fleet of 30 DC-9s operated by Iberia. Airlines large and small make up a family of operators that by early 1983 had ordered over 1,100 of these airliners, making them the most successful of the turbine powered aircraft produced by McDonnell Douglas.

History and Notes

The Douglas DC-9 was a completely new design with rear-mounted engines, the first prototype flying on 25 Feburary 1965. It was followed by the 80/90-seat Series 10, which was powered by Pratt & Whitney JT8D engines and entered service first with Delta Air Lines on 8 December 1965, production totalling 137. Next came the Series 30 with a fuselage lengthened by 14 ft 10¾ in (4.54 m) to seat up to 119 passengers, increased wing span and other improvements. They were used first by Eastern Air Lines on 1 February 1967.

· To meet the needs of SAS Douglas developed the Series 20, combining the Series 10 fuselage and increased-span wing of the Series 30; this entered service on 23 January 1969. SAS also inspired the high-capacity short-range Series 40 which entered service in March 1968. Derived from the Series 30, it has more fuel and a fuselage lengthened to seat up to 132 passengers. Last version is the Series 50, with a 'stretch' of 14 ft 3 in (4.34 m) to seat up to 139 passengers in a modernized interior, which entered service with Swissair in August 1975. All current versions are available in passenger (DC-9), cargo (DC-9F), convertible (DC-9CF) and passenger/cargo (DC-9RC) configurations. Military versions include the C-9A Nightingale and VC-9C transports of the USAF, and C-9B Skytrain II logistic transport of the US Navy. Orders and options for DC-9s total more than 1,100, of which all but about 5 per cent have been delivered.

Specification: Douglas DC-9 Series 50
Origin: USA
Type: short/medium-range transport
Accommodation: flight crew of 2; up to 139 passengers
Powerplant: two 15,500-lb (7031-kg) thrust Pratt & Whitney JT8D-15 turbofans
Performance: maximum speed 575 mph (925 km/h); economic cruising speed 510 mph (821 km/h); range with 97 passengers and fuel reserves 2,065 miles (3323 km)
Weights: empty 61,880 lb (28068 kg); maximum take-off 121,000 lb (54885 kg)
Dimensions: span 93 ft 5 in (28.47 m); length 133 ft 7¼ in (40.72 m); height 28 ft 0 in (8.53 m); wing area 1,000.75 sq ft (92.97 m²)

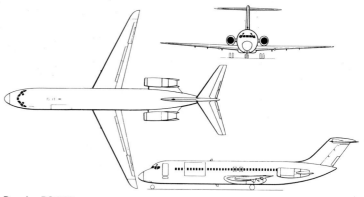

Douglas DC-9-30

Austrian Airlines, which began operating just over 25 years ago, in March 1958, was in early 1983 an exclusively Douglas DC-9 airline. This will change when it receives two Airbus A310-220s currently on order, but in the meantime AA can rely upon a fleet of 18 of these superb airliners: -30 (4), -50 (5) and -81 (9).

Douglas DC-9 Super 80 series

Construction of the first Douglas DC-9 began on 26 July 1963; in the 20 years since then this short/medium-range transport has proved a major success for the Douglas Aircraft Company. Growth since the Series 10 is shown by a gross weight increase from 77,700 lb (35244 kg) to 147,000 lb (66678 kg) for the Super 80.

History and Notes

Sales of more than 1,000 examples of the Douglas DC-9 represent a major success for the company in the commercial field. This was because the DC-9 appeared on the market some two years earlier than its main rival, the Boeing 737, and also because of its availability in a range of sizes and configurations. However, the company realized that with accelerating fuel costs a worthwhile market would exist for an improved DC-9-50 of greater capacity, with quieter more fuel-efficient engines. This, in effect, describes the DC-9 Super 81 and Super 82 which were certificated on 3 September 1980 and 30 July 1981 repectively.

Developed from the basic Series 50, the Super 81 has a wing increased in span by 14 ft 5 in (4.39 m), and a fuselage lengthened by 14 ft 3 in (4.34 m) to seat up to 172 passengers in a modern 'wide-look' cabin. Gross weight is increased by some 16 per cent, made possible by advanced-technology Pratt & Whitney JT8D series 200 turbofan engines. Not only are these more powerful than the earlier JT8Ds, they are quieter and have a better specific fuel consumption. The Super 82 is generally similar, but differs by having 20,000-lb (9072-kg) thrust JT8D-217 turbofans more suited to operation from 'hot and high' airports. The first Series 81 entered service with Swissair on its Zurich-London route on 5 October 1980. Orders and options total more than 100, and of these some 90 have been delivered.

Specification: Douglas DC-9 Super 81
Origin: USA
Type: short/medium-range transport
Accommodation: flight crew of 2; up to 172 passengers
Powerplant: two 18,500-lb (8391-kg) thrust Pratt & Whitney JT8D-209 turbofans
Performance: maximum speed 575 mph (925 km/h); cruising speed Mach 0.76; range with maximum fuel 3,060 miles (4925 km)
Weights: empty 79,757 lb (36177 kg); maximum take-off 140,000 lb (63503 kg)
Dimensions: span 107 ft 10 in (32.87 m); length 147 ft 10 in (45.06 m); height 29 ft 8 in (9.04 m); wing area 1,270.0 sq ft (117.98 m²)

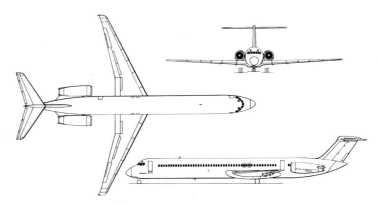

Douglas DC-9-80

One of the reasons for the sales success of the DC-9 is the fact that it has been made available in a range of variants to meet the requirements of various operators. The DC-9 Super 80 series has brought this fine airliner up-to-date, with advanced turbofan engines and the most modern interior furnishings and decor.

Perhaps better than most, this fine picture highlights the clean lines of a modern civil transport aircraft. Its swept wings, free from powerplant and engine nacelles, are able to produce optimum aerodynamic performance, and engines and tail surfaces are mounted in positions where the airflow is little disturbed.

Douglas DC-10

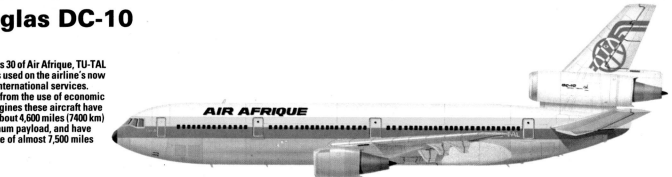

DC-10 Series 30 of Air Afrique, TU-TAL *Libreville,* is used on the airline's now extensive international services. Benefitting from the use of economic turbofan engines these aircraft have a range of about 4,600 miles (7400 km) with maximum payload, and have a ferry range of almost 7,500 miles (12070 km).

History and Notes

The Douglas Company began development of the DC-10 in March 1966, to meet a requirement of American Airlines for a wide-body transport. Despite competition, the DC-10 was ordered on 19 February 1968, and receipt of a second order in April 1968, from United Airlines, was a signal for production go-ahead. The initial Series 10 for domestic routes, with maximum seating for 380 passengers, was flown first on 29 August 1970, entering service with American Airlines on its Los Angeles-Chicago route on 5 August 1971.

Since then Douglas has developed a range of these transports, first being the Series 15 which is similar to the Series 10 but has more powerful CF6-50C2F engines and operates at a higher gross weight. The intercontinental-range Series 30 has wing span increased by 10 ft (3.05 m), an extra main wheel unit on the fuselage centreline, increased fuel and more powerful engines. The longer-range Series 30ER has even greater fuel capacity, and the intercontinental Series 40 (originally Series 20) differs from the Series 30 in having Pratt & Whitney engines. Model 10CF and 30CF convertible passenger/cargo versions are also available. The DC-10 was evaluated by the USAF for its Advanced Tanker/Cargo Aircraft requirement and its selection for this role was announced on 19 December 1977 under the designation KC-10A Extender, the first entering service on 17 March 1981.

Specification: Douglas DC-10 Series 30
Origin: USA
Type: commercial transport
Accommodation: flight crew of 3, up to 380 passengers
Powerplant: three 52,500-lb (23814-kg) thrust General Electric CF6-50C1 or -50C2 turbofans
Performance: maximum cruising speed 564 mph (908 km/h); normal cruising speed Mach 0.82; service ceiling 33,400 ft (10180 m); range with maximum payload 4,606 miles (7413 km)
Weights: empty 267,197 lb (121199 kg); maximum take-off 580,000 lb (263084 kg)
Dimensions: span 165 ft 4½ in (50.41 m); length 182 ft 1 in (55.50 m); height 58 ft 1 in (17.70 m); wing area 3,958.0 sq ft (367.70 m²)

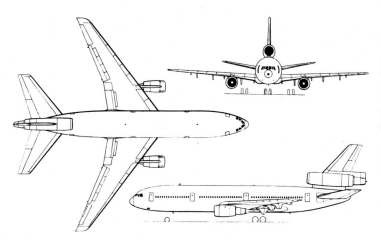

Douglas DC-10-30

Union de Transports Ariens (UTA) also operates a fleet of long-range DC-10 Series 30s. These find employment on this airline's routes from France to the African nations, Australia, the Far East, New Zealand, USA and other destinations. This picture shows clearly the extra main landing gear unit in the centre fuselage.

British Caledonian's DC-10 Series 30 G-BHDJ, seen here on approach, has one of the longest names carried by an airliner. This recognizes the ancestry of the founder of the McDonnell Company which merged with Douglas in 1967, its name being *James S. McDonnell – The Scottish American Aviation Pioneer.*

Douglas DC-10-30

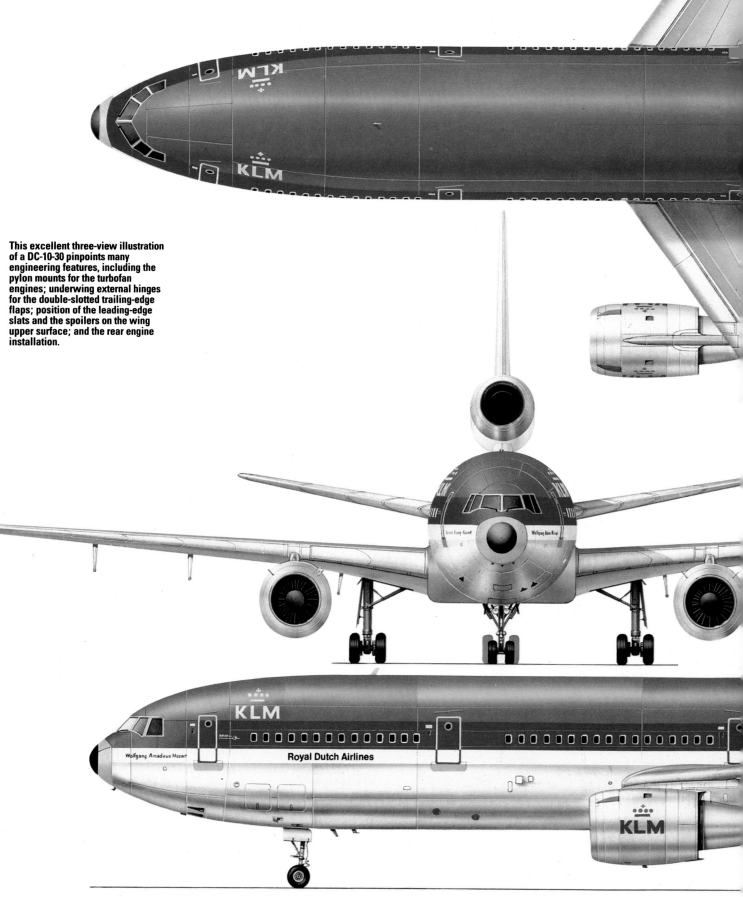

This excellent three-view illustration of a DC-10-30 pinpoints many engineering features, including the pylon mounts for the turbofan engines; underwing external hinges for the double-slotted trailing-edge flaps; position of the leading-edge slats and the spoilers on the wing upper surface; and the rear engine installation.

KLM

KLM

Wolfgang Amadeus Mozart

Royal Dutch Airlines

KLM

EMBRAER EMB-110 Bandeirante

This EMB-110C Bandeirante in service with Transportes Aereos de Bacia Amazonica (TABA) was one of the first of 10 EMB-110s now operated by this company. With services covering a large area of the vast Amazon region, TABA has found them valuable for service in an environment where reliability is essential.

History and Notes

The EMB-110 is numbered among several of the successful designs that have emanated from Empresa Brasileira de Aeronautica SA (usually abbreviated to EMBRAER) in Brazil. Evolved under guidance from the well-known French designer, Max Holste, the first of three YC-95 prototypes was flown on 26 October 1968. This is a cantilever low-wing monoplane with a conventional fuselage, swept tail surfaces and retractable tricycle landing gear and two Pratt & Whitney Aircraft of Canada PT6A turboprops in wing-mounted nacelles.

Civil transport versions include the EMB-110C, with basic seating for 15 passengers; the seven/eight-passenger EMB-110E(J) executive transport; the EMB-110P 18-passenger commuter; and the EMB-110P2 21-passenger commuter. There is also an EMB-110P1, a quick-change passenger/cargo variant of the EMB-110P2, and available since 1981 are the EMB-110P1/41 and EMB-110P2/41 higher gross weight versions of the P1 and P2 respectively. A pressurized EMB-110P3 to seat 19 passengers was in the design stage in 1982.

EMB-110 Bandeirantes are also in military use; specially equipped for such roles are the EMB-110P1SAR search and rescue aircraft and the EMB-111 maritime surveillance version, both of which are in service with the Brazilian air force under the respective designations of SC-95B and P-95.

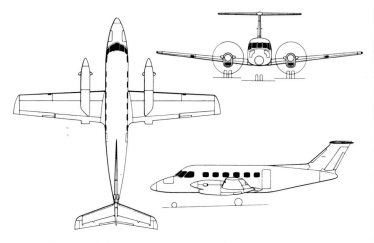

EMBRAER EMB-110P3 Bandeirante

This EMBRAER EMB-110P2 Bandeirante (Pioneer) of Air UK, which combined several UK operators, is one of the six (including two -110P1s) acquired by this company for its domestic and European services. A 21-passenger commuter with fuel-efficient turboprop engines, its sales are climbing towards the 500 mark.

Specification: EMBRAER EMB-110P2

Origin: Brazil
Type: commuter transport
Accommodation: flight crew of 2; up to 21 passengers
Powerplant: two 750-shp (559-kW) Pratt & Whitney Aircraft of Canada PT6A-34 turboprops
Performance: maximum cruising speed 257 mph (414 km/h) at 8,000 ft (2440 m); economic cruising speed 208 mph (335 km/h) at 10,000 ft (3050 m); service ceiling 22,500 ft (6860 m); range with fuel reserves 1,243 miles (2000 km)
Weights: empty equipped 7,837 lb (3555 kg); maximum take-off 12,500 lb (5670 kg)
Dimensions: span 50 ft 3½ in (15.33 m); length 49 ft 6½ in (15.10 m); height 16 ft 1¾ in (4.92 m); wing area 313.23 sq ft (29.10 m²)

EMBRAER EMB-120 Brasilia

The larger-capacity EMBRAER EMB-120 Brasilia, scheduled to enter service in 1984, inherits many features of the successful Bandeirante. It introduces a swept T-tail and a lengthened, pressurized fuselage. This will permit optimum cruising performance at double the altitude of the EMB-110, with even better fuel economy.

History and Notes

Encouraged by successful penetration of the commuter market by its EMB-110 Bandeirante, EMBRAER initiated in September 1979 design studies for a completely new pressurized twin-turbo civil transport to seat a maximum of 30 passengers. It is anticipated that future developments will include corporate and all-cargo versions, as well as maritime patrol and ECM versions for military use.

A mock-up of the passenger EMB-120 was displayed at Rio de Janeiro in the spring of 1980 and its design was finalized in 1982. Prototype construction has been initiated, the first being due to fly during July 1983, and it is planned to gain certification to US FAR Pt 25 during 1984. Configured as a cantilever low-wing monoplane with a circular-section pressurized fuselage, a T-tail with all swept surfaces, and retractable tricycle landing gear with twin wheels on each unit, the EMB-120 is to be powered by two Pratt & Whitney Aircraft of Canada PW115 (formerly PT7A) turboprops. This is a new advanced-technology turboprop that has been developed for 30/40-passenger short-haul transports. It is claimed that it will provide a 20 per cent improvement in specific fuel consumption by comparison with current turboprop engines in this class.

EMBRAER has received options on approximately 115 Brasilias, these coming from 23 operators in eight countries.

Specification: EMBRAER EMB-120 Brasilia
Origin: Brazil
Type: short-range utility transport
Accommodation: flight crew of 2; up to 30 passengers
Powerplant: two 1,500-shp (1119-kW) Pratt & Whitney Aircraft of Canada PW115 turboprops
Performance: (estimated) maximum cruising speed 337 mph (542 km/h); economic cruising speed 290 mph (467 km/h); service ceiling 32,000 ft (9755 m); range with 30 passengers and fuel reserves 628 miles (1010 km)
Weights: (estimated): empty operating 12,295 lb (5577 kg); maximum take-off 21,165 lb (9600 kg)
Dimensions: span 64 ft 10¾ in (19.78 m); length 64 ft 8½ in (19.72 m); height 21 ft 8 in (6.60 m); wing area 409.31 sq ft (38.02 m²)

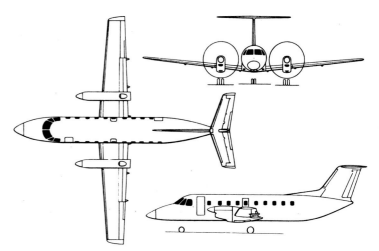

EMBRAER EMB-120 Brasilia

The EMB-120 Brasilia mockup shown below gives a preview of its clean lines. It will also have a well-equipped interior and the aircraft systems will include air conditioning, duplicated hydraulics, and pneumatic wing and tailplane leading-edge de-icing as standard. A wide range of optional advanced avionics is planned.

Fokker F.27 Friendship

Fokker's F.27 Friendship has graced the world's airways for over a quarter of a century; in so doing it has earned for itself many friends, including aircrew, passengers and maintenance personnel. Air Tanzania numbers several Friendships in its fleet, used mainly for domestic and regional scheduled passenger services.

History and Notes

Fokker built many fine airliners during the 'between-wars' years, and soon after the end of World War II began looking at the needs of the European airlines. This led to the P.275 design for a 32-seat transport, but by 1952 this had been developed to the larger F.27 with a pressurized fuselage.

A first prototype (PH-NIV) flew on 24 November 1955, powered by Rolls-Royce Dart 507 turboprops. A second prototype, with Dart 511 engines and a lengthened fuselage to seat 32 passengers, was flown on 31 January 1957. Between these dates Fokker concluded arrangements with Fairchild in the USA to build and market the F.27 in North America, resulting in the Fairchild F-27/FH-227.

Fokker production versions comprise the 40/52-seat F.27 Friendship Mk 100 and Mk 200, differing only in powerplant; similar passenger/cargo Mk 300 and Mk 400 Combiplane versions; the Mk 500, a lengthened-fuselage (by 4 ft 11 in/1.50 m) Mk 200 to seat 52/60 passengers; the Mk 600, basically a Mk 200 with large cargo door; and a single Mk 700, a Mk 600 with Mk 100 powerplant. There are also the military Mk 400M and 500M, the Mk 400M aerial survey and, for maritime patrol, the F.27 Maritime. Fokker F.27 sales exceed 530 with some 300 now in service; major operators include Air France, Air New Zealand, Air UK, Ansett Airlines, LADE, Libyan Arab Airlines, Malaysian Airlines System, PIA and Trans Australia Airline.

Specification: Fokker F.27 Mk 200
Origin: Netherlands
Type: medium-range transport
Accommodation: flight crew of 2; up to 48 passengers
Powerplant: two 2,280-eshp (1700-ekW) Rolls-Royce Dart Mk 536-7R turboprops
Performance: normal cruising speed 298 mph (480 km/h) at 20,000 ft (6095 m); service ceiling 29,500 ft (8990 m); range with 44 passengers and fuel reserves 1,197 miles (1926 km)
Weights: empty operating 26,480 lb (12011 kg); maximum take-off 45,000 lb (20412 kg)
Dimensions: span 95 ft 2 in (29.00 m); length 77 ft 3½ in (23.56 m); height 27 ft 10½ in (8.50 m); wing area 753.50 sq ft (70.00 m²)

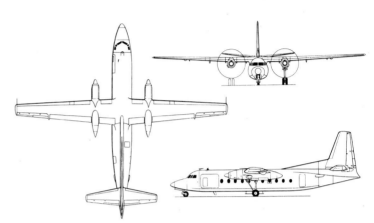

Fokker F.27 Friendship 500

Features of the Fokker F.27 Friendship design include a circular-section pressurized fuselage, retractable tricycle landing gear and pneumatic de-icing as standard for wing and tail unit leading-edges. Rolls-Royce Dart turboprop engines have been standard from the outset, now with four-blade constant-speed propellers.

This picture of a Fokker F.27-100 Friendship gives a good impression of the large diameter of its circular-section fuselage and tall fin. This fuselage provides a cabin with a maximum width of 8 ft 2 in (2.49 m) and which, in the case of the Srs 500, is 52 ft 4 in (15.95 m) in length excluding the flight deck.

Fokker F.28 Fellowship

Although inheriting many structural features of the F.27, Fokker's F.28 Fellowship is far more modern in appearance. This is a result of its clean swept wings, rear-mounted turbofan powerplant and T-tail with swept surfaces. The wing incorporates double-slotted Fowler flaps, and five upper-surface lift dumpers on each wing.

History and Notes

Foreseeing a market for a higher-performance airliner with more capacity than the F.27, Fokker began in 1960 the design of a turbofan-powered short/medium-range transport to complement the F.27. Later designated F.28 Fellowship, this airliner entered production in 1964 with backing from the Netherlands government and risk-sharing partners in West Germany and the UK. Of low-wing monoplane configuration, the F.28 has a circular-section pressurized fuselage, T-tail with swept surfaces, retractable tricycle landing gear and rear-mounted Rolls-Royce Spey turbofans. The first prototype (PH-JHG) was flown on 9 May 1967 and the F.28 entered service on 24 February 1969.

Current versions in 1983 include the Mk 3000, and Mk 4000 with a fuselage lengthened by 7 ft 3 in (2.21 m), seating up to 65 and 85 passengers respectively; the Mk 3000 is available optionally with a 15-seat executive layout. The earlier Mk 1000 and Mk 2000 were respective equivalents of the current production aircraft; the Mk 6000 (2 built) has a standard lengthened fuselage combined with a 4 ft (1.22 m) increase in wing span. Projected Mk 5000 (short fuselage/increased span wings) and Mk 6600 (still longer fuselage) versions were not built.

More than 190 F.28s have been sold and major operators include Linjeflyg AB, Airlines of Western Australia and Garuda Indonesian Airways.

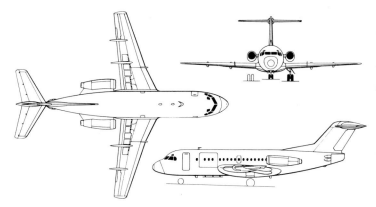

Fokker F.28 Fellowship 1000

Specification: Fokker F.28 Mk 3000
Origin: Netherlands
Type: short/medium-range transport
Accommodation: flight crew of 2; up to 65 passengers
Powerplant: two 9,900-lb (4491-kg) thrust Rolls-Royce RB.183-2 Spey Mk 555-15P turbofans
Performance: maximum cruising speed 523 mph (842 km/h) at 23,000 ft (7010 m); economic cruising speed 421 mph (678 km/h) at 30,000 ft (9145 m); maximum range with 65 passengers and fuel reserves 1,969 miles (3169 km)
Weights: empty operating 36,994 lb (16780 kg); maximum take-off 72,995 lb (33110 kg)
Dimensions: span 82 ft 3 in (25.07 m); length 89 ft 10¾ in (27.40 m); height 27 ft 9½ in (8.47 m); wing area 850.38 sq ft (79.00 m²)

Right: Well known in European skies are the F.27 and F.28 aircraft of Nederlandse Luchtvaart Maatschappij (NLM), which is a subsidiary of the Dutch national airline KLM. NLM's City Hopper air services link European, Channel islands and British cities and towns, but there is no doubt over which nation this Fellowship is operating.

The Swedish domestic airline Linjeflyg has an all-Fellowship fleet of some 13 aircraft. The majority of these are F.28 Series 4000s, which provide a maximum seating capacity of 85. They are used extensively on internal services throughout the nation, and are used also by Linjeflyg for charter operations.

Government Aircraft Factories Nomad

The Australian Government Aircraft Factories N22 Nomad follows simple and basic lines for a short-haul transport, adopting a typical high-set wing configuration to give maximum cabin volume. P2-DNL illustrated is no longer operated by Papua's Douglas Airways, but two other Nomads are retained in service.

History and Notes

Australia's Government Aircraft Factories began development in the late 1960s of a small turboprop-powered STOL transport for civil and military use, and the first of two N2 prototypes (VH-SUP) was flown on 23 July 1971. A strut-braced high-wing monoplane, the N2 has a rectangular-section fuselage mounting a low-set stub wing, to which the upper wing bracing struts are attached, and which also incorporates fairings for the main units of the retractable tricycle landing gear; the tail unit is conventional and power is provided by two Allison turboprops in wing-mounted nacelles.

Versions of the aircraft, named Nomad, have included the initial production N22 with seats for up to 12 passengers, and the N24 with a fuselage lengthened by 3 ft 9 in (1.14 m) to seat a maximum of 15. Production versions in 1982 included the 13-passenger N22B and 17-passenger N24A. An N22F Floatmaster was certificated with float landing gear in the USA during 1979, and with amphibious floats in 1980. There is also a short-fuselage military version which has the name Missionmaster, a coastal patrol Searchmaster B and a more extensively equipped Searchmaster L. By early 1982 Nomad sales of all versions were in excess of 150, but it was announced later in the year that production was to end in 1984 after the completion of 170 aircraft. Australian operators include Bush Pilots Airways, Clubair Pty, H.C. Sleigh Airlines and Skywest Airlines Pty.

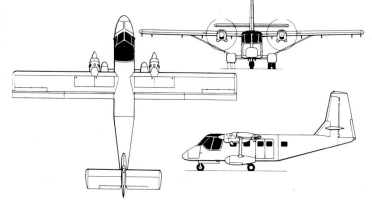

GAF Nomad N22

Specification: GAF Nomad N24A
Origin: Australia
Type: STOL utility transport
Accommodation: flight crew of 1 or 2; 17 or 16 passengers respectively
Powerplant: two 420-shp (313-kW) Allison 250-B17C turboprops
Performance: cruising speed 193 mph (311 km/h); service ceiling 20,000 ft (6095 m); range with fuel reserves 840 miles (1352 km) at 10,000 ft (3050 m)
Weights: empty operating 5,241 lb (2377 kg); maximum take-off 9,200 lb (4173 kg)
Dimensions: span 54 ft 2¼ in (16.52 m); length 47 ft 1¼ in (14.36 m); height 18 ft 1½ in (5.52 m); wing area 324.0 sq ft (30.10 m²)

Polynesian Airlines, based on Western Samoa, provides island-linking services in mid-Pacific. Places with fascinating names like Fiji, Tahiti and Tonga know the sound of Polynesian's aircraft, its small and varied fleet including one GAF N22B Nomad (5W-FAR *Apaula*); at the other extreme it has one Boeing 737 (5W-PAL).

Grumman G-73 Mallard

The only non-military product built by Grumman in the post-war period, the G-73 Mallard was quite sophisticated for its era. Its two-compartment cabin was ideal to provide luxurious accommodation for those who required it, and one of the post-war production aircraft served as a personal transport for the King of Egypt.

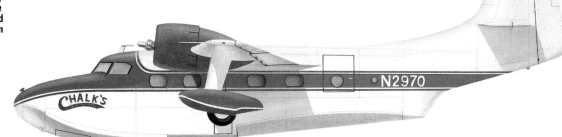

History and Notes

After the end of World War II Grumman began design and development of a twin-engined civil amphibian flying-boat. It benefitted from considerable experience gained by the company in the design and large-scale construction of military flying-boats. Given the designation G-73 and the name Mallard, the new aircraft was a high-wing monoplane of all-metal construction, with a stressed-skin two-step hull, upswept at the rear to mount a conventional but tall tail unit. Retractable tricycle landing gear provided the amphibious capability and balancer floats, rigidly mounted beneath the wings, served also as auxiliary fuel tanks, each of 50-US gal (189-litre) capacity. Power was provided by two Pratt & Whitney R-1340 Wasp radial engines in wing-mounted nacelles, each driving three-blade variable-pitch propellers. A separate flight deck was provided for the aircrew but the main accommodation, for 10 passengers seated in two compartments, was not only well appointed, but was air-conditioned, heated, soundproofed and provided with baggage compartments fore and aft.

Comparatively small numbers of these aircraft, remain in service now, Chalk's International Airline of Miami, Florida, being the major operator, a nostalgic airline (founded in 1918) with equally nostalgic aircraft. With the Mallard Chalk's operates scheduled passenger services between Miami, Bimini, Cat Cay, Chub Cay and Nassau.

Specification: Grumman G-73 Mallard
Origin: USA
Type: light amphibian flying-boat
Accommodation: flight crew of 2; up to 10 passengers
Powerplant: two 600-hp (447-kW) Pratt & Whitney R-1340-S3H1 Wasp radial piston engines
Performance: maximum speed 215 mph (346 km/h); cruising speed 180 mph (290 km/h) at 8,000 ft (2440 m); service ceiling 23,000 ft (7010 m); range with maximum fuel 1,380 miles (2221 km)
Weights: empty 9,350 lb (4241 kg); maximum take-off 12,750 lb (5783 kg)
Dimensions: span 66 ft 8 in (20.32 m); length 48 ft 4 in (14.73 m); height, on landing gear 18 ft 9 in (5.72 m); wing area 444.0 sq ft (41.25 m²)

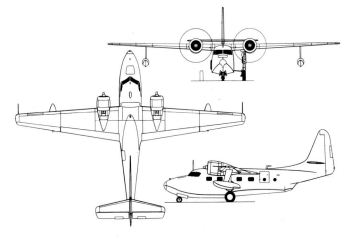

Grumman Mallard

Amphibians and flying-boats are a diminishing category of aircraft, represented here by a Grumman Mallard operated by Chalk's International Airline of Miami, Florida. The post-war G-73 Mallard was derived from the slightly smaller and successful Grumman G-21 Goose which saw considerable service in World War II.

Gulfstream Aerospace G-159C Gulfstream I-C

Air North of South Burlington, Vermont, has a small fleet of aircraft that provide scheduled commuter and freight services over a wide area. The airline operates two Gulfstream G-ICs, N159AN illustrated in this profile and N160AN, these being the largest capacity aircraft that are used by this company.

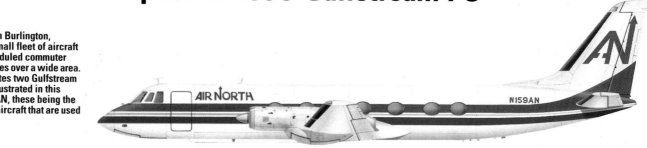

History and Notes

In the mid-1950s Grumman began the design of a twin-turboprop executive transport intended to accommodate a crew of two and 10 to 14 passengers; an alternative high-density seating layout could seat 24. In this form the aircraft was designated G-159 Gulfstream I, a cantilever low-wing monoplane with a circular-section pressurized fuselage, conventional tail unit with swept surfaces, retractable tricycle landing gear and power provided by two Rolls-Royce Dart turboprops in wing-mounted nacelles. The prototype was flown for the first time on 14 August 1958 and gained certification on 21 May 1959. When production ended in 1969, Grumman had built 200 of these aircraft.

Company re-organization has led to Gulfstream American Corporation being responsible for support of this aircraft from September 1978, and in early 1979 this company began to investigate the feasibility of developing a 'stretched' version for the commuter airline market. A prototype conversion of a Gulfstream I (N5400C), its fuselage lengthened by 10 ft 8 in (3.25 m) to seat up to 37 passengers and with room for a galley, baggage compartments and toilet, was flown first on 25 October 1979 with the revised designation G159C Gulfstream I-C. Comparatively few conversions had been completed by the spring of 1983, but examples of this commuter airliner are operated by Air North, Air US and Chaparral Airlines.

Specification: Gulfstream Aerospace G159C Gulfstream I-C
Origin: USA
Type: commuter transport
Accommodation: flight crew of two; up to 37 passengers
Powerplant: two 1,990-eshp (1484-ekW) Rolls-Royce Dart Mk 529-8X turboprops
Performance: maximum cruising speed 355 mph (571 km/h); certificated ceiling 30,000 ft (9145 m); range with maximum payload and fuel reserves 500 miles (805 km)
Weights: empty 23,693 lb (10747); maximum take-off 36,000 lb (16329 kg)
Dimensions: span 78 ft 4 in (23.88 m); length 75 ft 4 in (22.96 m); height 23 ft 0 in (7.01 m); wing area 610.30 sq ft (56.70 m²)

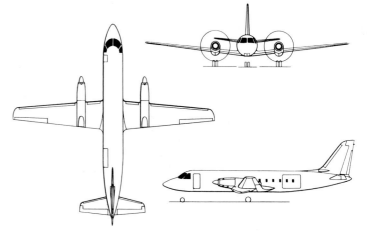

Gulfstream Aerospace Gulfstream I

Gulfstream Aerospace Corporation, formerly Gulfstream American Corporation, is continuing to support and develop the Gulfstream line of executive/commuter aircraft. Illustrated is the prototype G-159C Gulfstream I-C, a lengthened version of the Grumman G-159 Gulfstream I 19-seat executive aircraft.

Gulfstream Aerospace Gulfstream II/II-B

Although of smaller size, development of the Grumman Gulfstream from the Mk I to Mk II version followed the same pattern as that of the Fokker F.27/F.28. Wing-mounted Dart turboprops gave place to rear-mounted Spey turbofans, the wings became swept, and the conventional tail unit was replaced by a swept T-tail.

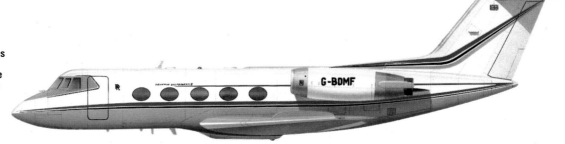

History and Notes

Grumman market research indicated the need for an aircraft with the Gulfstream I's capacity combining better short-field and long-range performance. In 1976 the company began studies for a turbofan-engined version of the Gulfstream I; a full-scale mock-up was built, attracting 30 firm orders, and on 5 May 1965 the programme was given a go-ahead. The first aircraft made its maiden flight on 2 October 1966, and the type entered service in early 1968. The new Gulfstream II differed considerably from its predecessor, having swept wings, a T-tail with swept surfaces, and engines in rear-mounted nacelles. These last were Rolls-Royce Speys, installed in an airframe some 35 per cent lighter than the similarly-powered BAC (BAe) One-Eleven and Fokker F.28, which meant the Gulfstream II could easily meet its performance requirements. Later improvements added engine hush-kits and tiptanks to extend range, but production ended after 258 were built. By then, Gulfstream American was supporting this aircraft and in 1980 announced that the advanced wing developed for the Gulfstream III, was to be available for retrofit to Gulfstream IIs, the resulting conversion being designated Gulfstream II-B. The first was flown on 17 March 1981, this wing offering increased range and greater fuel efficiency. By mid-1982 the company had received firm orders for 26 Gulfstream II-B conversions.

Specification: Gulfstream Aerospace Gulfstream II-B
Origin: USA
Type: executive transport
Accommodation: flight crew of 2; up to 19 passengers
Powerplant: two 11,400-lb (5171-kg) thrust Rolls-Royce Spey Mk 511-8 turbofans
Performance: economic cruising speed Mach 0.71; certificated ceiling 45,000 ft (13715 m); range with 8 passengers and fuel reserves 4,088 miles (6579 km)
Weights: empty operating 39,100 lb (17735 kg); maximum take-off 68,200 lb (30935 kg)
Dimensions: span 77 ft 10 in (23.72 m); length 79 ft 11 in (24.36 m); height 24 ft 6 in (7.47 m); wing area 934.66 sq ft (86.83 m²)

Gulfstream Aerospace Gulfstream II

Grumman's Gulfstream programme became owned by Gulfstream American (now Gulfstream Aerospace) Corporation. This company continued to develop the Gulfstream III and the advanced wing for this latter aircraft, incorporating wingtip winglets, is available for the Gulfstream II, the conversion known as the Gulfstream IIB.

Gulfstream Aerospace Gulfstream III

The winglets incorporated in the advanced wing of the Gulfstream III were developed by the US National Aeronautics & Space Administration (NASA). By reducing the energy lost to wingtip vortices they contribute to overall efficiency in cruising flight. This wing is also available as a retrofit for the Gulfstream II.

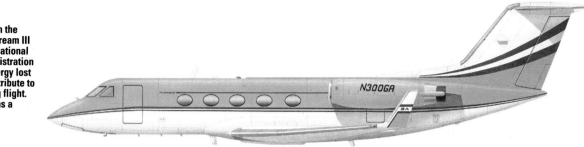

History and Notes

Grumman first announced its intention to develop the Gulfstream III in November 1976, but the programme was suspended temporarily in the spring of 1977. When it was resumed in 1978, it was by the newly formed Grumman American Aviation Corporation, now Gulfstream Aerospace. Derived from the Gulfstream II, the first Gulfstream III was converted from a Gulfstream II (construction number 249) taken from the production line. It differed by having the fuselage 'stretched' by 3 ft 11 in (1.19 m) to allow the introduction of a revised nose, windscreen and lengthened cabin. More importantly it introduced a new supercritical wing incorporating NASA (Whitcomb) wingtip winglets that were intended to improve fuel economy and efficiency. Wing span was also increased by 9 ft (2.74 m) to provide a total integral fuel capacity of 4,192 US gal (15868 litres).

First flown on 2 December 1979 and certificated on 22 September 1980, the Gulfstream III has since demonstrated superb performance from this re-design. In addition to establishing a number of course records and straight line and distance records. During 8-10 January 1982 a new round-the-world class record of 47 hours 39 minutes was set at an average 489.3 mph (787.5 km/h). From orders totalling 130, about 70 have been delivered. They include three equipped for long-range maritime patrol which are used by the Royal Danish air force.

Specification: Gulfstream Aerospace Gulfstream III
Origin: USA
Type: executive/utility transport
Accommodation: flight crew of 2 or 3; up to 19 passengers
Powerplant: two 11,400-lb (5171-kg) thrust Rolls-Royce Spey Mk 511-8 turbofans
Performance: economic cruising speed Mach 0.77; certificated ceiling 45,000 ft (13715 m); range with maximum fuel and reserves 4,200 miles (6759 km)
Weights: empty operating 38,000 lb (17237 kg); maximum take-off 68,200 lb (30935 kg)
Dimensions: span 77 ft 10 in (23.72 m); length 83 ft 1 in (25.32 m); height 24 ft 4½ in (7.43 m); wing area 934.66 sq ft (86.83 m²)

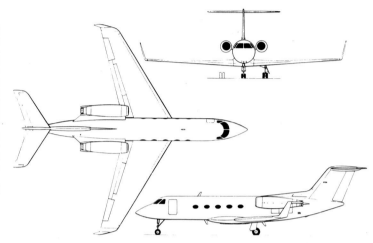

Gulfstream Aerospace Gulfstream III

The Gulfstream Aerospace Gulfstream III which, by comparison with the Gulfstream II, differs primarily by introducing an advanced wing incorporating wingtip winglets. These, combined with fuel efficient Rolls-Royce Spey turbofan engines and increased fuel capacity, give extended range and sparkling performance.

Handley Page H.P.R.7 Herald

A total of only 50 Handley Page Heralds was built before production ended. That illustrated in this profile, G-BAZJ of Air UK, is a Herald 200 which was the major production version. This operator, providing passenger and cargo services within the UK and to points in Europe, is now the major user of Heralds.

History and Notes

The Handley Page H.P.R.7 Herald medium-range transport prototype (G-AODE) made its first flight on 25 August 1955. A cantilever high-wing monoplane with a circular-section pressurized fuselage, the Herald had a conventional tail unit, retractable tricycle landing gear, and power provided by four 870-hp (649-kW) Alvis Leonides radial engines in wing-mounted nacelles.

Handley Page had expected the Herald to sell to operators in more remote areas, and its easy-to-maintain airframe and powerplant were slanted to such a market. The Herald failed to gain interest, however, for by mid-1955 the capability, reliability and economy of turboprop engines had been demonstrated by aircraft such as the Vickers Viscount. A decision was made in May 1957 to develop a Dart-powered version and only the two prototypes were flown with piston engines, being converted subsequently to turbine power. Produced first was the Herald Series 100 (4 built) which seated 47 passengers; it was followed by the 'stretched' fuselage (by 3 ft 7 in/1.09 m) Series 200 (38 built) to seat 56. Production ended with eight Series 400 military variants for the Royal Malaysian air force, no further examples being built after collapse of the Handley Page company in 1970. Of the 30 Heralds which now remain in airline service almost half of them are operated by Air UK.

Specification: Handley Page H.P.R.7 Herald Series 200
Origin: UK
Type: medium-range transport
Accommodation: flight crew of 2; up to 56 passengers
Powerplant: two 2,105-eshp (1570-ekW) Rolls-Royce Dart 527 turboprops
Performance: maximum cruising speed 274 mph (441 km/h) at 15,000 ft (4570 m); economic cruising speed 265 mph (426 km/h) at 23,000 ft (7010 m); service ceiling 27,900 ft (8505 m); range with maximum payload 1,110 miles (1786 km)
Weights: empty operating 25,800 lb (11703 kg); maximum take-off 43,000 lb (19504 kg)
Dimensions: span 94 ft 9 in (28.88 m); length 75 ft 6 in (23.01 m); height 24 ft 1 in (7.34 m); wing area 886.00 sq ft (82.31 m²)

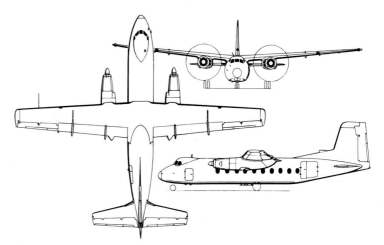

Handley Page H.P.R.7 Herald Series 200

Once seen by Handley Page as an important aircraft for the company, with very considerable sales potential, development of the H.P.R.7 Herald was delayed by a mid-course change from piston-engined to turboprop powerplant. As a result, by the time it was certificated its market no longer existed.

Ilyushin Il-14 'Crate'

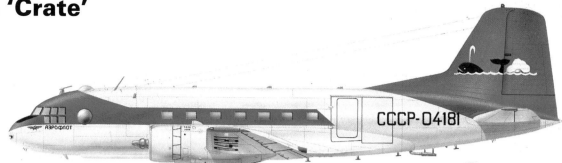

Ilyushin's Il-14 short-range transport is no longer produced, but many of these reliable aircraft continue in service, used by Aeroflot and CAAC, national airline of the People's Republic of China. It has the distinction of being the first civil transport to be built in the Soviet Union after the end of World War II.

History and Notes

In the years immediately following World War II, Aeroflot leaned heavily upon ex-military Douglas C-47s and Lisunov Li-2s (licence-built Douglas DC-3s) for its post-war domestic services. However, it was clear that a DC-3 replacement could not be delayed indefinitely, and Ilyushin began the design and construction of the Il-12 short-range transport, which was first flown in early 1946.

A conventional low-wing monoplane with retractable tricycle landing gear and two wing-mounted radial engines, the Il-12 was superseded in 1954 by the improved Il-14 with a number of refinements, including wings of more efficient aerofoil section and more powerful engines. Production versions have included the Il-14P (passenger) seating 18 passengers; and the Il-14M (modified) with a 3 ft 3¼ in (1.00 m) fuselage 'stretch' to seat 24; high-density layouts introduced in 1958 allowed Il-14P and Il-14Ms to seat 24 and 36 passengers respectively. Il-14T and Il-14G cargo versions, with double doors on the port side, are believed to relate respectively to the Il-14P and Il-14M versions. Soviet production of civil and military Il-14s totalled about 3,500 aircraft, of which just under 300 now remain in service, the majority operated by Aeroflot, and CAAC in China. Small numbers were also licence-built by Avia in Czechoslovakia (Avia 14) and VEB Flugzeugwerke in East Germany (VEB Il-14P).

Specification: Ilyushin Il-14M

Origin: USSR
Type: short-range transport
Accommodation: flight crew of 5; up to 36 passengers
Powerplant: two 1,900-hp (1417-kW) Shvetsov ASh-82T radial piston engines
Performance: maximum cruising speed 217 mph (350 km/h) at 9,840 ft (3000 m); economic cruising speed 199 mph (320 km/h) at 9,840 ft (3000 m); service ceiling 24,280 ft (7400 m); range with maximum payload and fuel reserves 249 miles (400 km)
Weights: empty equipped 27,778 lb (12600 kg); maximum take-off 38,581 lb (17500 kg)
Dimensions: span 104 ft 0 in (31.70 m); length 73 ft 2¼ in (22.31 m); height 25 ft 7 in (7.80 m); wing area 1,076.43 sq ft (100.00 m²)

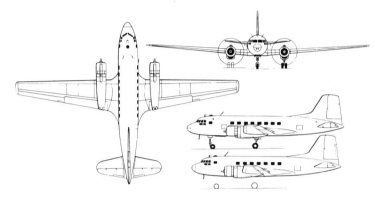

Ilyushin Il-14M (lower side view: Il-14P)

It is believed that most of the large number of Ilyushin Il-14s built in the Soviet Union were used in military service, primarily as cargo or troop transports, but some were used also in a VIP transport role. A number were presented by the Soviet Union for personal use by the heads of state of friendly nations.

Ilyushin Il-18 'Coot'

So far as the Soviet Union is concerned, the Ilyushin Il-18 was built in comparatively small numbers, but almost half of the total remain in service. While Aeroflot and CAAC are the major user, Interflug, the national airline of the German Democratic Republic, has a fleet of about 15, almost half used as cargo carriers.

Ilyushin Il-18

History and Notes

Aeroflot's need for a medium-range civil transport with greater capacity than the Il-14 led to design of the Il-18, a low-wing monoplane with a circular-section pressurized fuselage, conventional tail unit, retractable tricycle landing gear, and power provided by four wing-mounted 4,000-eshp (2983-ekW) Kuznetsov SN-4 turboprops. The prototype (CCCP-L5811) was flown first on 4 July 1957.

The initial production Il-18s, introduced into service by Aeroflot on 20 April 1959, had seats for 75 passengers. Subsequent versions with layouts revised for up to 84 and 100 passengers were the Il-18B and Il-18V respectively, the latter having some cabin windows repositioned. More extensively developed was the Il-18D (known initially as the Il-18I) with increased fuel tankage, more powerful engines and 'warm weather' seats for up to 122 passengers; this extra capacity was gained by using the large storage area needed for passengers' outer garments during the Russian winter; with its onset, seating capacity reverted to 110. The Il-18E was a generally similar version, but without the additional fuel capacity. About 700 were built, small numbers entering military service, and about 300 remained in airline use in early 1982, the major operators being Aeroflot and CAAC.

Specifically military versions include an ECM or Elint aircraft and an ASW Il-38 which have the NATO reporting names 'Coot-A' and 'May' respectively.

Specification: Ilyushin Il-18D
Origin: USSR
Type: medium/long-range transport
Accommodation: flight crew of 5; up to 122 passengers
Powerplant: four 4,250-eshp (3169-ekW) Ivchenko AI-20M turboprops
Performance: maximum cruising speed 419 mph (675 km/h); maximum operating ceiling 32,810 ft (10000 m); range with maximum payload and fuel reserves 2,299 miles (3700 km)
Weights: empty equipped 77,162 lb (35000 kg); maximum take-off 141,096 lb (64000 kg)
Dimensions: span 122 ft 8½ in (37.40 m); length 117 ft 9½ in (35.90 m); height 33 ft 4½ in (10.17 m); wing area 1,507.00 sq ft (140.00 m²)

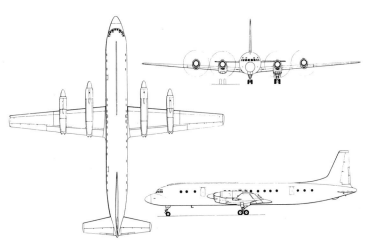

Ilyushin Il-18

In the same way that Western nations have converted some transports for use in military roles, the Ilyushin Il-18 is being used by the Soviet air force. An ECM or Elint *'Coot-A'* version has been reported, with fuselage pods for avionics or cameras, and an ASW/maritime patrol *'May'*, which seems similar to the US Navy's P-3 Orion.

Ilyushin Il-62 'Classic'

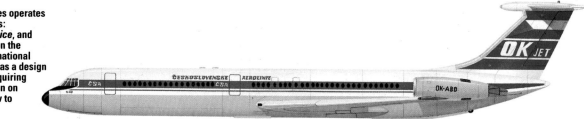

CSA Czechoslovak Airlines operates a number of Ilyushin Il-62s: illustrated is OK-ABD *Kosice*, and these aircraft are in use on the airline's long-range international routes. Such capability was a design specification, Aeroflot requiring these aircraft for operation on services such as Moscow to Montreal or New York.

History and Notes

First announced on 24 September 1962, the Ilyushin Il-62 long-range airliner was designed for use over routes such as Moscow-New York, a distance of some 4,800 miles (7725 km). The prototype (CCCP-06156) was first flown in January 1963, and was a low-wing monoplane with swept wings and tail surfaces, a circular-section pressurized fuselage, retractable tricycle landing gear, and four engines mounted in pairs on each side of the rear fuselage. As first flown the Il-62 was powered by 16,535-lb (7500-kg) thrust Lyulka AL-7 turbojets, but soon afterwards the aircraft was flown with the Kuznetsov turbofans for which it was designed. Passenger accommodation is in two cabins, with maximum seating for 186: 72 forward and 114 rear.

Il-62s entered service with Aeroflot in early 1967, and following initial use on domestic services was introduced on the airline's Moscow-Montreal route on 15 September 1967, then representing the Soviet Union's first long-range four-engine intercontinental jet transport. An improved Il-62M entered service in 1974, incorporating many refinements and more powerful, more fuel efficient Soloviev D-30KU turbofan engines. The most recent version, first announced in 1978, has structural strengthening for operation at higher gross weights, de-rated engines, and a cabin layout for a maximum 195 passengers. About 190 Il-62s now remain in airline service, approximately 75 per cent with Aeroflot.

Specification: Ilyushin Il-62M

Origin: USSR
Type: long-range transport
Accommodation: flight crew of 5; up to 174 passengers
Powerplant: four 25,353-lb (11500-kg) thrust Soloviev D-30KU turbofans
Performance: cruising speed at optimum altitude 510-553 mph (820-890 km/h); range with maximum payload and fuel reserves 4,847 miles (7800 km)
Weights: empty operating 153,001 lb (69400 kg); maximum take-off 363,763 lb (165000 kg)
Dimensions: span 141 ft 8¾ in (43.20 m); length 174 ft 3¼ in (53.12 m); height 40 ft 6¼ in (12.35 m); wing area 3,037.67 sq ft (282.20 m²)

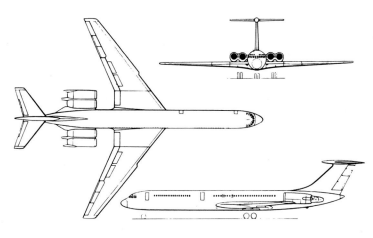

Ilyushin Il-62M

The interior of the Ilyushin Il-62 has a basic two cabin layout; in the Il-62 and Il-62M the forward and rear cabins seat 66 and 102 respectively in an economy class layout. The Il-62MK introduced in 1978 has, like many airliners of other nations, been given a modern interior that gives a more spacious appearance.

Ilyushin Il-76 'Candid'

This profile of an Ilyushin Il-76T emphasizes the graceful lines of this large, long-range transport which has both civil and military applications. The designation Il-76M applies to the military version in service with the Soviet Air Force and, reportedly, Czechoslovakia, Iraq and Poland.

Ilyushin Il-76

History and Notes

In the late 1960s Ilyushin began design studies of a heavy transport aircraft required by Aeroflot for operation in Siberian regions. Designated Il-76, a prototype (CCCP-86712) was flown for the first time on 25 March 1971, and this was exhibited later that year at the Paris Air Show. It has a high-set monoplane wing (to ensure maximum internal capacity) mounted above a circular-section pressurized fuselage, a T-tail with all-swept surfaces, and retractable tricycle landing gear that has a four-wheel nose unit and two main units each with eight wheels. Thus it has 20 wheels with low-pressure tyres to distribute the aircraft's weight over a maximum surface area and, to enhance operational potential, tyre pressures can be adjusted in flight. Power is provided by four Soloviev turbofan engines in underwing pods. The all-important loading operations take place via two large clamshell type doors, an upward hinged panel and a downward-hinged loading ramp being incorporated in the upswept rear fuselage.

Production Il-76Ts began to enter service with Aeroflot in early 1983, and in 1982 this airline was probably operating between 50 and 60; others serve with Iraqi Airways, Libyan Arab Airlines and Syrianair. An Il-76M military transport, of which about 140 are believed to be in service with the Soviet air force, differs by having a rear turret. The type is also being evaluated for use in AWACS and inflight-refuelling tanker roles.

Specification: Ilyushin Il-76T
Origin: USSR
Type: medium/long-range freight transport
Accommodation: flight crew of 7
Powerplant: four 26,455-lb (12000-kg) thrust Soloviev D-30KP turbofans
Performance: maximum speed 528 mph (850 km/h); cruising speed 466-497 mph (750-800 km/h); range with maximum payload 3,107 miles (5000 km)
Weights: maximum payload 88,185 lb (40000 kg); maximum take-off 374,786 lb (170000 kg)
Dimensions: span 165 ft 8¼ in (50.50 m); length 152 ft 10¼ in (46.59 m); height 48 ft 5 in (14.76 m); wing area 3,229.28 sq ft (300.00 m²)

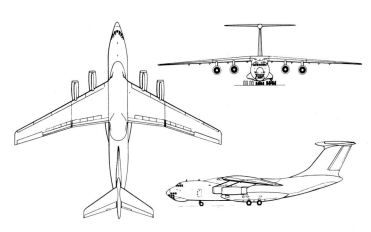

Ilyushin Il-76

Ilyushin Il-76T YI-AIL illustrated is one of a number operated by Iraqi Airways on its long-distance international routes. Aeroflot continues as the major operator of the type with about 50 in use, but about 30 were in service with airlines in Africa and the Middle East in early 1983.

Ilyushin Il-86 'Camber'

CCCP-86000 illustrated in this profile was the first prototype of Ilyushin's Il-86, the first wide-body transport to be developed in the Soviet Union. From reports in early 1983 it would seem that Aeroflot may have as many as 50 in service, but that those for the Polish airline LOT had not then been delivered.

History and Notes

A first intimation that the Soviet aerospace industry was developing a wide-body transport came at the 1971 Paris Air Show. Little was then known of its proposed configuration, but the first pictures of the Ilyushin Il-86 prototype (CCCP-86000), which made its maiden flight on 22 December 1976, showed it to be similar to the European Airbus Industrie A300 except for having four instead of two underwing-mounted turbofan engines, and for having a third main landing gear unit similar to that of the Douglas DC-10 Series 30 and 40. The Il-86 has accommodation for a maximum of 350 passengers, split between three cabins which are separated by wardrobes. Access to this aircraft is unique, being via three lower-deck airstair type doors which enable the aircraft to dispense with conventional airport loading/unloading bridges. These airstairs reach down to ground level and, after boarding, passengers can deposit their baggage in lower-deck stowage positions before climbing one of three fixed internal staircases to the passenger cabins.

What is believed to be the initial production aircraft flew on 24 October 1977, but it was not until 24 September 1979 that Aeroflot took delivery of its first Il-86. Scheduled services were started on 26 December 1980, initially between Moscow and Tashkent. About 50 are believed to be in service, but so far as is known a small batch for the Polish airline LOT has not yet been delivered.

Specification: Ilyushin Il-86
Origin: USSR
Type: medium-range transport
Accommodation: flight crew of 5; up to 350 passengers
Powerplant: four 28,660-lb (13000 kg) thrust Kuznetsov NK-86 turbofans
Performance: (estimated) cruising speed 559-590 mph (900-950 km/h) at optimum altitude; range with 88,185 lb (40000 kg) payload 2,237 miles (3600 km)
Weights: maximum payload 92,594 lb (42000 kg); maximum take-off 454,152 lb (206000 kg)
Dimensions: span 157 ft 8¼ in (48.06 m); length 195 ft 4 in (59.54 m); height 51 ft 10½ in (15.81 m); wing area 3,444.56 sq ft (320.00 m²)

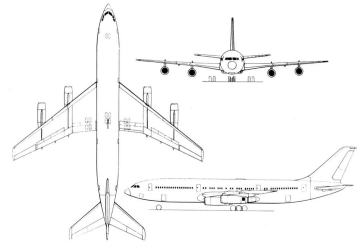

Ilyushin Il-86

Showing some similarity to, and having the same medium-range role as the initial European A-300 Airbus, Ilyushin's Il-86 wide-body transport is identified easily by its four-turbofan powerplant. It is reported that, as has been the case with the Airbus, a long-range version of the Il-86 is under development.

Israel Aircraft Industries IAI 101/102/201/202 Arava

IAI 101B Arava, which is intended mainly for the US commuter market, and where it is sold as the Cargo Commuterliner. Illustrated is N701AE, one of 10 ordered by the new US operator Airspur, which it will use for cargo traffic. Its passenger operation is to be carried out by Westland 30 helicopters.

History and Notes

In 1966 Israel Aircraft Industries designed a light STOL transport for civil and military use. The prototype IAI 101 (4X-IAI), named Arava, made its first flight on 27 November 1969, but the October War of 1973 meant that development was switched from the civil 101 to the IAI 201 military transport. As a result, the first production civil transport, based on the IAI 101 prototype, was not certificated until April 1976.

Of braced high-wing monoplane configuration, the Arava has its wing mounted above a circular-section fuselage pod; the wing serves also to mount two turboprop engines. Twin booms extend aft from the engine nacelles, carrying twin fins and rudders, the booms being united at the rear by the tailplane. The fuselage mounts fixed tricycle landing gear. The initial IAI 102 civil production version seats up to 20 passengers in airline-standard seating, but is suitable also for a wide range of uses. An updated IAI 101B, intended primarily for the US commuter market, was certificated in the USA in November 1980. Marketed there as the Cargo Commuterliner, it can seat 18 passengers or carry a 4,000-lb (1814-kg) load of cargo with maximum fuel. An advanced IAI 202 is also available, its fuselage pod lengthened by 2 ft 11¾ in (0.91 m) to seat 24 passengers in civil applications. Total sales of Aravas now exceed the 100 mark, the principal markets being Africa, South America and the USA.

Specification: IAI 202 Arava
Origin: Israel
Type: STOL commuter/utility transport
Accommodation: flight crew of 2; up to 24 passengers
Powerplant: two 750-shp (559-kW) Pratt & Whitney Aircraft of Canada PT6A-36 turboprops
Performance: maximum cruising speed 198 mph (319 km/h) at 10,000 ft (3050 m); service ceiling 25,000 ft (7620 m); range with maximum payload 392 miles (631 km)
Weights: empty operating 8,816 lb (3999 kg); maximum take-off 15,000 lb (6804 kg)
Dimensions: span 68 ft 9 in (20.96 m); length 42 ft 9 in (13.03 m); height 17 ft 1 in (5.21 m); wing area 470.18 sq ft (43.68 m²)

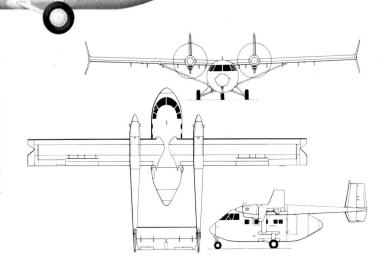

Israel Aircraft Industries IAI 202 Arava

The lines of the Israel Aircraft Industries Arava, plus its fixed tricycle landing gear, might suggest an archaic design. This is far from the case, as it is intended for multi-role use and to be easy to maintain. Its high-set braced wing ensures maximum space in the cabin for passengers or freight.

Let L-410 Turbolet

CCCP-67176 illustrated in Aeroflot insignia is a Let L-410UVP Turbolet, which is the current production version. The wing incorporates advanced high-lift features such as double-slotted flaps and spoilers, and has bank control surfaces which extend automatically on the appropriate wing if an engine fails.

History and Notes

In 1966 Let initiated the design of a twin-turboprop light transport at its plant at Kunovice, Czechoslovakia. The first L-410 prototype was flown on 19 April 1969, powered by two 715-eshp (533-ekW) United (now Pratt & Whitney) Aircraft of Canada PT6A-27 turboprop engines. In configuration the L-410 is a cantilever high-wing monoplane with a conventional tail unit and retractable tricycle landing gear, the main units retracting into external fairings on each side of the lower fuselage. The PT6A-27 powerplant was retained for three further prototypes, the 27 initial production L-410As built during 1971-4 and for a single L-410AF aerial survey aircraft built and supplied to Hungary in 1974.

Before L-410A manufacture ended an improved L-410M was under development, the first of 109 production examples being delivered in 1976. In addition to incorporating some refinements, it is powered by indigenous Walter M-601A turboprops. Currently being built is the L-410UVP, this differing in having a fuselage lengthened by 1 ft 6½ in (0.47 m), increases in wing span and fin and rudder area, and improved instrumentation and systems. The L-410's basic layout is as a civil airliner, but the type can be readily equipped for a variety of uses, and operate from surfaces such as grass, sand and gravel strips or, with skis, from ice and snow. Already operating with Aeroflot, it is expected to be used on a large scale for internal feederline services.

Specification: Let L-410UVP Turbolet
Origin: Czechoslovakia
Type: utility transport
Accommodation: flight crew of 2; up to 15 passengers
Powerplant: two 730-eshp (544-ekW) Walter M-601B turboprops
Performance: maximum cruising speed 227 mph (365 km/h) at 9,840 ft (3000 m); economic cruising speed 186 mph (300 km/h); range with maximum payload and fuel reserves 286 miles (460 km)
Weights: empty equipped 8,378 lb (3800 kg); maximum take-off 12,566 lb (5700 kg)
Dimensions: span 63 ft 11 in (19.48 m); length 47 ft 5¾ in (14.47 m); height 19 ft 1½ in (5.83 m); wing area 378.69 sq ft (35.18 m²)

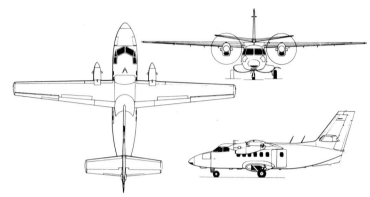

Let L-410 UVP Turbolet

Produced by Let at Kunovice in Czechoslovakia, the L-410 Turbolet is expected to become standard equipment on the internal feederline operations of the Russian airline Aeroflot. However, only comparatively small numbers were in service in early 1983. Its roomy cabin has a maximum width of 6 ft 4¾ in (1.95 m).

Lockheed L-188 Electra

Typical of the all-cargo conversions of Lockheed Electras carried out by Lockheed Aircraft Services, that of Great Northern illustrated in the profile shows clearly the large cargo door. Measuring 6 ft 8 in by 11 ft 3 in (2.03 m by 3.43 m), the conversion included strengthening and a new heavy-duty floor.

History and Notes

In early 1955 American Airlines required a medium-range airliner for domestic use and Lockheed was successful in gaining a contract for 35 of its L-188 Electra design. A second order, from Eastern Air Lines for 40 aircraft, was sufficient to launch production. A cantilever low-wing monoplane with a circular-section fuselage, conventional tail unit and retractable tricycle landing gear, the first prototype (N1881) was flown on 6 December 1957. The initial production L-188A entered service with Eastern Air Lines on 12 January 1959, followed later that year by the L-188C with increased fuel capacity to extend range.

By then Lockheed had a backlog of orders and seemed set for a long production run, but the loss of two aircraft in inexplicable circumstances brought imposition of speed restrictions until the cause was established. The investigation resulted in structural strengthening, introduced on the production line and retrospectively to in-use aircraft. However, it was not until January 1961 that the speed limitation was lifted and by then Lockheed had lost its market. Production ended after 170 had been built and Lockheed Aircraft Services later modified 41 for use in cargo/passenger or all-cargo roles. About 80 remain in service, the major operators being Varig Brazilian Airlines and Zantop International Airlines.

Specification: Lockheed L-188A Electra
Origin: USA
Type: short/medium-range transport
Accommodation: flight crew of 2 or 3; up to 99 passengers
Powerplant: four 3,750-eshp (2796-ekW) Allison 510-D13A turboprops
Performance: maximum cruising speed 405 mph (652 km/h) at 22,000 ft (6705 m); economic cruising speed 374 mph (602 km/h); service ceiling 27,000 ft (8230 m); range with maximum payload 2,200 miles (3541 km)
Weights: empty operating 61,500 lb (27896 kg); maximum take-off 116,000 lb (52617 kg)
Dimensions: span 99 ft 0 in (30.18 m); length 104 ft 6 in (31.85 m); height 32 ft 10 in (10.01 m); wing area 1,300.0 sq ft (120.77 m²)

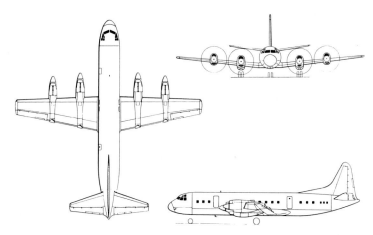

Lockheed L-188 Electra

Operating truly 'on the road to Mandalay', this Lockheed L-188A Electra of Mandala Airlines (PK-RLF *Rengga Gading*) leads a busy life on services in East and West Indonesia. For 15 years this airline has depended on the reliability of these aircraft, and the DC-3s and Viscounts that form its fleet.

The third member of the current family of US wide-body turbine-powered transports, Lockheed's L-1011 TriStar adopts the same three-engine layout as the McDonnell Douglas DC-10. The company's original prototype (N1011) became known as the Advanced TriStar and was used to develop new techniques, equipment and systems.

Lockheed L-1011 TriStar

Saudi Arabian Airlines operates a fleet of 17 L-1011-200 TriStars, and there were an additional 220 in worldwide service in early 1983. However, financial losses in the production of these aircraft, and a continuing recession in the air transport scene, will close the TriStar production line during 1984.

History and Notes

Lockheed's L-1011 TriStar was designed to meet the same American Airlines' requirement that had initiated production of the Douglas DC-10, to which the TriStar is generally similar in configuration, including the disposition of its three-engined powerplant. Production began in early 1968, after orders for 144 aircraft had been received, and the first was flown on 17 November 1970. At this point both Lockheed in the USA and Rolls-Royce in the UK ran into serious economic problems, requiring assistance from their respective governments and the renegotiation of contracts before production could be resumed, and it was not until 14 April 1972 that certification was gained, with the first scheduled service flown by Eastern Air Lines on 26 April 1972.

This basic TriStar was designated L-1011-1 and was powered by three 42,000-lb (19051-kg) thrust Rolls-Royce RB.211-22B turbofans. It was followed by an extended-range L-1011-100 with increased fuel tankage, and later by an extended-range L-1011-200 with more powerful RB.211-524 engines giving improved performance for operation in 'hot and high' areas. Orders for all versions, including the L-1011-500, now total 247, and of this number some 240 have been delivered. Production is due to end in 1984 after the delivery of all outstanding orders.

Specification: Lockheed L-1011-200 TriStar
Origin: USA
Type: commercial transport
Accommodation: flight crew of 3; up to 400 passengers
Powerplant: three 48,000-lb or 50,000-lb (21772-kg or 22680-kg) thrust Rolls-Royce RB.211-524 or -524B/B4 turbofans respectively
Performance: maximum cruising speed 605 mph (974 km/h) at 30,000 ft (9145 m); economic cruising speed 553 mph (890 km/h) at 35,000 ft (10670 m); range with maximum passengers and fuel reserves 4,145 miles (6671 km)
Weights: empty operating 248,400 lb (112672 kg); maximum take-off 466,000 lb (211374 kg)
Dimensions: span 155 ft 4 in (47.35 m); length 177 ft 8½ in (54.17 m); height 55 ft 4 in (16.87 m); wing area 3,456.0 sq ft (321.06 m²)

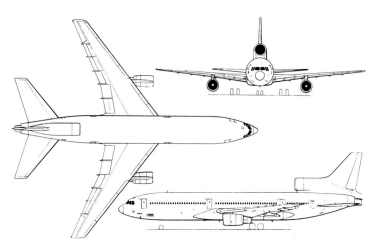

Lockheed L-1011-1 TriStar

The first of the wide-body turbine-powered transports to be developed by the Lockheed company, the L-1011 TriStar entered service on 26 April 1972. Air Canada is one of the major users, its 18 in service including eight L-1011-1s, four extended-range L-1011-100s, and six long-range L-1011-500s.

Lockheed L-1011-500 and Advanced TriStar

Pan Am operates 12 Lockheed L-1011-500 TriStars. The aircraft, which entered service first with British Airways on 7 May 1979, adopted the range extension techniques used by Boeing for the 747SP. Thus the shortened-fuselage, lower-capacity and reduced-weight structure is able to carry 5,140 US gallons (119774 litres) of extra fuel.

History and Notes

It was intended that when testing of the first TriStar (N1011) had ended it should be refurbished to airline standards. However, the company found a need to retain it for development and it has since become known as the Advanced TriStar. It has modifications and equipment that includes active aileron control, an all-moving tailplane, automatic brakes, automatic take-off thrust, extended wingtips and advanced avionics and systems. Added to the starboard side of the instrument panel in late 1981 were three full-colour CRT displays to test pilot reactions and evaluate different information formats.

Airline interest in a long-range version of the TriStar led to the L-1011-500, which began flight tests in October 1978. It differs from early production versions by having a shorter fuselage (by 13 ft 6 in/4.11 m), reducing internal seating to a maximum of 330 passengers. This smaller payload allows for increased fuel, carried in added centre-section tanks. There are also variations in interior layout, and the extended wingtips/active ailerons tested on the Advanced TriStar became standard on the L-1011-500 in 1981. Major operators of TriStars of all versions are Air Canada, All Nippon, British Airways, Delta Air Lines, Eastern Air Lines, Saudia and TWA.

Specification: Lockheed L-1011-500 TriStar
Origin: USA
Type: long-range commercial transport
Accommodation: flight crew of 3; up to 330 passengers
Powerplant: three 50,000-lb (22680-kg) thrust Rolls-Royce RB.211-524B/B4 turbofans
Performance: maximum cruising speed 605 mph (974 km/h) at 30,000 ft (9145 m); economic cruising speed 553 mph (890 km/h) at 35,000 ft (10670 m); service ceiling 43,000 ft (13105 m); range with maximum passengers and fuel reserves 6,154 miles (9904 km)
Weights: empty operating 245,400 lb (111312 kg); maximum take-off 510,000 lb (231332 kg)
Dimensions: span 164 ft 4 in (50.09 m); length 164 ft 2½ in (50.05 m); height 55 ft 4 in (16.87 m); wing area 3541.0 sq ft (328.96 m²)

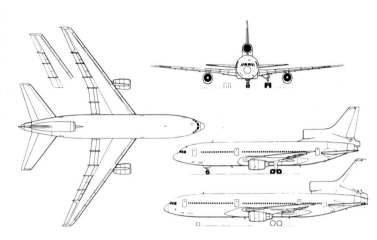

Lockheed L-1011-500 TriStar (lower side and scrap views: L-1011-100)

L-1011-500 TriStars introduced the extended wingtips/active ailerons developed on the Advanced Tristar. Increased span can, under gust or manoeuvring conditions, cause unacceptable structural loads. The active ailerons deflect automatically to offset such loads, avoiding a need for wing structure redesign or strengthening.

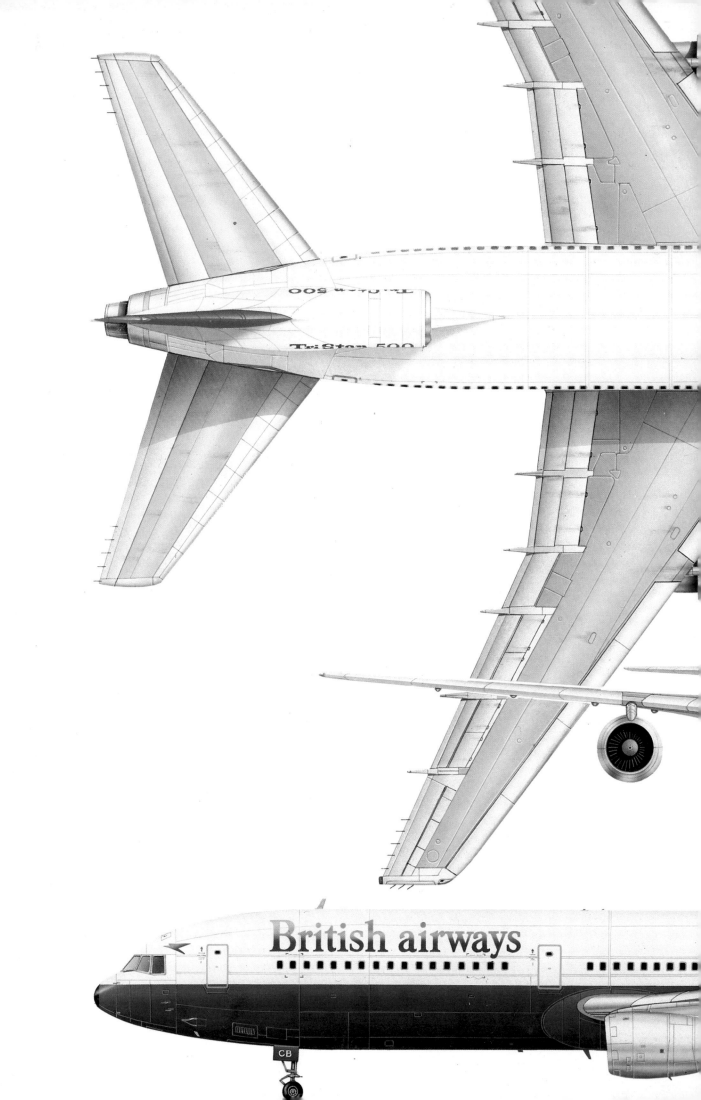

The British Airways' Lockheed
L-1011-500 TriStar G-BFCB, named
The Harry Wheatcroft Rose,
recognizing one of Britain's best-
known rose-growers. The illustration
shows the basic circular section of
the fuselage, and the comprehensive
range of high-lift devices
incorporated in the wing structure:
all controls are powered.

Lockheed Model 1329 JetStar I/II

Iraqi Airways was one of a number of airlines that found Lockheed's JetStar light transport a useful addition to their fleets. Its 10-passenger capacity make it valuable for many charter and/or commuter operations, especially when it is realized that both versions have a full payload range of about 2,000 miles (3219 km).

History and Notes

In March 1957 Lockheed announced the development of a turbojet-powered light transport, of which the prototype flew on 4 September 1957. It was configured as a low-wing monoplane with swept wing, a pressurized fuselage, conventional tail unit with swept surfaces and retractable tricycle landing gear, and was powered by two Bristol Siddeley Orpheus turbojets, mounted one on each side of the rear fuselage. An unusual feature was the inclusion of large streamlined external fuel tanks, but Lockheed wanted to ensure the new Model 1329 JetStar would be fast and long-ranged.

The Orpheus engines of the prototypes were replaced by four 2,400-lb (1089-kg) thrust Pratt & Whitney JT12A-6 turbojets, mounted two on each side of the rear fuselage, in the initial production version. Uprated JT12A-6As followed in 1963 and JT12A-8s in 1967. The JetStar was replaced by an improved JetStar II after certification on 14 December 1976, with a number of refinements and a change of powerplant to Garrett TFE 731 turbofans, the earlier models then becoming known as JetStar Is. Production of JetStar Is totalled 162, and 40 JetStar IIs had been built when production was suspended in 1980 and it seems unlikely that this will be resumed. Deliveries of JetStar Is included 16 for the USAF as C-140A (5) and VC-140B (11), and a number of JetStar Is and IIs serve with airlines, Iraqi Airways, (as an example) having six JetStar IIs.

Specification: Lockheed JetStar II
Origin: USA
Type: light utility transport
Accommodation: flight crew of 2; up to 10 passengers
Powerplant: four 3,700-lb (1678-kg) thrust Garrett TFE 831-3 turbofans
Performance: maximum cruising speed 547 mph (880 km/h) at 30,000 ft (9145 m); service ceiling 43,000 ft (13105 m); range with maximum payload and fuel reserves 2,995 miles (4820 km)
Weights: empty operating 24,900 lb (11294 kg); maximum take-off 44,500 lb (20185 kg)
Dimensions: span 54 ft 5 in (16.59 m); length 60 ft 5in (18.41 m); height 20 ft 5 in (6.22 m); wing area 542.5 sq ft (50.40 m²)

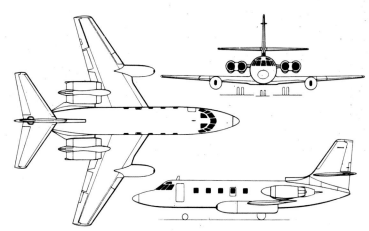

Lockheed 1329-25 JetStar II

In addition to use by airlines, Lockheed's Model 1329 JetStar was of suitable capacity to make it popular as an executive transport aircraft, acquired by many business concerns for such use. The standard interior had a wardrobe, galley and toilet aft of the cabin, with baggage compartments fore and aft.

Martin 4-0-4

Only about 14 Martin 4-0-4s remained in airline service in early 1983, all in North and South America. Aerolineas Dominicanas (ADSA) retained two in its small fleet, HI-285 shown in the accompanying illustration. Marco Island Airways of Marco Island, Florida, retains five for mainland/island-linking routes.

History and Notes

The Glenn L. Martin Company announced in November 1945 the development of a 36/40-seat transport designated Martin 2-0-2. This was of low-wing monoplane configuration with an unpressurized circular-section fuselage, conventional tail unit, retractable tricycle landing gear and two Pratt & Whitney Double Wasp radial engines. The prototype flew on 22 November 1946, was the first twin-engined airliner of US post-war design to gain certification (in August 1947) and entered service in October. However, after a few months one was lost in strange circumstances, leading to investigations that pinpointed some weakness in the structure. No further examples of the Model 2-0-2 were built as such, and those in service were modified by structural strengthening.

Before these events, Martin had proposed new passenger and cargo versions of the 2-0-2 as the Martin 3-0-3 and 3-0-4 respectively. Instead, an improved Martin 4-0-4 was built, introducing a slightly lengthened (by 3 ft 3 in/0.99 m) pressurized fuselage and detail improvements. Construction reached 103 before production ended in early 1953, supplied to Eastern Air Lines (60), TWA (41), plus two for the US Coast Guard as RM-1s. These aircraft have since changed hands many times and about 14 of them now remain in service with Marco Island Airways and Provincetown-Boston Airlines as the major operators.

Specification: Martin 4-0-4
Origin: USA
Type: short/medium range transport
Accommodation: flight crew of 3 or 4; up to 40 passengers
Powerplant: two 2,400-hp (1790-kW) Pratt & Whitney R-2800-CB16 Double Wasp radial piston engines
Performance: maximum speed 312 mph (502 km/h); cruising speed 280 mph (451 km/h); service ceiling 29,000 ft (8840 m); range with maximum payload 1,080 miles (1738 km)
Weights: empty equipped 29,126 lb (13211 kg); maximum take-off 44,900 lb (20366 kg)
Dimensions: span 93 ft 3 in (28.42 m); length 74 ft 7 in (22.73 m); height 28 ft 5 in (8.66 m); wing area 864.0 sq ft (80.27 m²)

Martin 4-0-4

Like many early post-World War II civil transports for which high hopes were once entertained by the originating company, the Martin 4-0-4 was to be built in only small numbers. An unpressurized, piston engined design, it was unable to meet the competition offered by the new generation of turboprop-powered airliners.

Mil Mi-8 'Hip'

The Mil Mi-8 is available in three civil versions. These comprise the basic Mi-8 passenger version seating 28-32; a utility Mi-8T primarily for freight, but able to have 24 tip-up seats in the cabin; or the de luxe Mi-8 Salon which seats 11 passengers as standard in luxury accommodation and can carry a hostess and buffet.

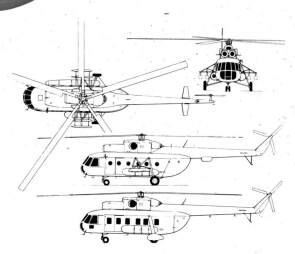

History and Notes

The Mil bureau began design in 1960 of a transport helicopter then identified as the V-8; this was later designated Mi-8 and flew for the first time in prototype form during 1961. It was of fairly conventional helicopter configuration, the pod-and-boom fuselage carried on non-retractable tricycle landing gear, but the main and anti-torque tail rotors were powered by a 2,700-shp (2013-kW) Soloviev turboshaft engine. The considerable power output of this unit made it possible to design a cabin/fuselage much larger than any produced earlier by the bureau.

In 1983 this robust and reliable helicopter continues in large-scale production, benefitting from refinements introduced during more than 20 years of construction. The most significant was the installation of two Isotov turboshaft engines to replace the single Soloviev engine of early production aircraft. The standard passenger version is designated Mi-8 (NATO reporting name 'Hip-C'), but there is also a utility Mi-8T and the de luxe Mi-8 Salon. Large numbers of Mi-8s are used by Aeroflot and production is believed to have reached the 8,000 mark, but the majority of these are in military service. They include an assault transport (NATO reporting name 'Hip-C'); an ECM version ('Hip-D'); an armed helicopter, reportedly the world's most heavily armed ('Hip-E') and a similar export version ('Hip-F').

Specification: Mil Mi-8 'Hip-C'
Origin: USSR
Type: transport helicopter
Accommodation: flight crew of 2 or 3; up to 32 passengers
Powerplant: two 1,700-shp (1268-kW) Isotov TV2-117A turboshafts
Performance: maximum speed 155 mph (250 km/h) at sea level; maximum cruising speed 140 mph 9225 km/h); service ceiling 14,765 ft (4500 m); range with 28 passengers and fuel reserves 311 miles (500 km)
Weights: empty 14,991 lb (6800 kg); maximum take-off 25,507 lb (11570 kg)
Dimensions: main rotor diameter 69 ft 10½ in (21.30 m); length, rotors turning 82 ft 9¾ in (25.24 m); height 18 ft 6½ in (5.65 m); main rotor disc area 3,832.08 sq ft (356.00 m²)

Mil Mi-8 'Hip' (lower side view: civil version)

Right: This superb picture of a Mil Mi-8 helicopter shows many design features, but also emphasizes the robust construction of the modern rotary-wing aircraft. One can also begin to appreciate the pugnacious appearance of the military Mi-8s which, when fully equipped with external weapons, are indeed a fighting machine.

Below: The very capable Mil Mi-8 is the only such helicopter flying in the West, being owned by Asahi Helicopter in Japan. Aeroflot, the Russian airline, flies many Mi-8s, but the major proportion of the 8,000-plus built so far are in service with the military.

NAMC YS-11

Major user of the NAMC YS-11 is Japan's Toa Domestic Airlines which, in early 1983 had a fleet of 39. Only 182 YS-11s were built before production ended, but with their Rolls-Royce Dart turboprop engines they have gained a reputation for reliability that is important for high-density island-hopping operations.

History and Notes

In May 1957 a Transport Aircraft Development Association was created in Japan to design a medium-range civil airliner. With this task completed the Nihon Aircraft Manufacturing Company (NAMC) was established on 1 June 1959 as a management and sales medium to co-ordinate the activities of the six member companies which were to build the components for this YS-11 aircraft. They comprised Fuji, Kawasaki, Mitsubishi, Nippi, Shin Meiwa and Showa, with Mitsubishi responsible also for final assembly.

Activities began with the construction of two prototypes, the first being flown on 30 August 1962. Certification was gained on 25 August 1964 and production deliveries began in March 1965. In configuration the YS-11 is a low-wing monoplane with a circular-section pressurized fuselage, retractable tricycle landing gear and two wing-mounted turboprops. Initial production version was the YS-11-100, followed by three similar versions certificated at a higher gross weight, comprising YS-11A-200 passenger, YS-11A-300 mixed passenger/cargo, and YS-11A-400 all-cargo versions. Subsequently, equivalent YS-11A-500, YS-11A-600, and YS-11A-700 versions became available with the maximum take-off weight increased by 1,102 lb (500 kg). Production ended in 1974 after 182 aircraft had been built, and of this total about 120 remain in service with Airborne Express, All Nippon Airways and Toa Domestic as major operators.

Specification: NAMC YS-11A-200
Origin: Japan
Type: short/medium-range transport
Accommodation: flight crew of 2; up to 60 passengers
Powerplant: two 3,060-eshp (2282-ekW) Rolls-Royce Dart Mk 542-10K turboprops
Performance: maximum cruising speed 291 mph (468 km/h) at 15,000 ft (4670 m); economic cruising speed 281 mph (452 km/h) at 20,000 ft (6095 m); service ceiling 22,900 ft (6980 m); range with maximum payload 680 miles (1094 km)
Weights: empty operating 33,993 lb (15419 kg); maximum take-off 54,013 lb (24500 kg)
Dimensions: span 104 ft 11¾ in (32.00 m); length 86 ft 3½ in (26.30 m); height 29 ft 5½ in (8.98 m); wing area 1,020.45 sq ft (94.80 m²)

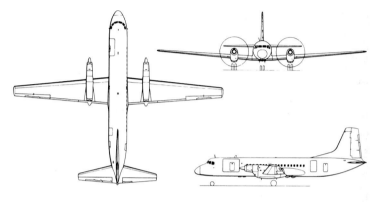

NAMC YS-11

More than half of the 117 NAMC YS-11s in service in early 1983 were operated by airlines in Japan. Of this total, 25 were included in the large fleet of aircraft that makes All Nippon the largest airline in Japan. The majority of them are YS-11As, which are certificated for operation at a higher gross weight.

Piper PA-31 Navajo/Chieftain series

Rather more than 500 Navajo/
Chieftain aircraft were in service
with commuter airlines in early 1983,
although N39CA shown in this profile
has since been re-sold by Chaparral
Airlines. The basic Chieftain airframe
has been used by the company in the
development of its T-1020 and T-1040
specialized commuter aircraft.

History and Notes

Anxious to gain a share of the corporate/commuter aircraft market that had already been tapped by Beech Aircraft Corporation, Piper flew the first example of the twin-engined PA-31 Navajo in September 1964. A cantilever low-wing monoplane with a conventional tail unit, retractable tricycle landing gear and wing-mounted engines, the Navajo seats a pilot and seven passengers. The Navajo proved a successful aircraft and versions developed in addition to the basic model include the Turbo Navajo with turbocharged engines, the Navajo C/R with counter-rotating propellers and the Pressurized Navajo: the last sold in only small numbers and was withdrawn in 1977. In current production is the Navajo, now with 310-hp (231-kW) turbocharged engines as standard and the Navajo C/R with 325-hp (242-kW) counter-rotating turbocharged engines.

The PA-31-350 Chieftain, introduced in 1972, is a lengthened-fuselage version of the Navajo (by 2 ft 0 in/0.61 m) with more powerful counter-rotating turbocharged engines. It is produced in Standard and Commuter versions, seating six and 10 passengers respectively, and has a reinforced cabin floor to make it suitable also for cargo carrying. About 500 Chieftains are currently serving with commuter airlines.

Specification: Piper PA-31-350 Chieftain
Origin: USA
Type: corporate/commuter transport
Accommodation: flight crew of 1 or 2 with 11 or 10 passengers respectively
Powerplant: two 350-hp (261-kW) Avco Lycoming LTIO/TIO-540-J2BD flat-six counter-rotating turbocharged piston engines
Performance: maximum cruising speed 254 mph (409 km/h) at 20,000 ft (6095 m); economic cruising speed 199 mph (320 km/h) at 12,000 ft (3660 m); certificated altitude 24,000 ft (7315 m); maximum range with fuel reserves 1,484 miles (2388 km)
Weights: empty 4,221 lb (1915 kg); maximum take-off 7,000 lb (3175 m)
Dimensions: span 40 ft 8 in (12.40 m); length 34 ft 7½ in (10.55 m); height 13 ft 0 in (3.96 m); wing area 229.0 sq ft (21.27 m²)

Piper PA-31-350 Chieftain

Piper Aircraft Corporation has gained a fair degree of success in the commuter aircraft market which it entered in the mid-1960s. This was based initially on the twin-engined PA-31 Navajo, but gained greater momentum when the PA-31-350 Chieftain, as illustrated here, was first introduced in 1972.

Piper PA-31T Cheyenne I-II/PA-42 Cheyenne III

The sleek exterior lines of the Piper PA-42 Cheyenne III are complemented by a high standard of interior equipment. It is pressurized, air-conditioned and has an automatic environmental control system. Also provided as standard is an oxygen system and a complete de-icing system for airframe and engines.

History and Notes

On 20 August 1969 Piper flew the prototype of a new six/eight-seat pressurized transport named as the PA-31T Cheyenne. Similar in configuration and appearance to the Navajo from which it was developed, the Cheyenne differed in one important respect: it was the first aircraft designed by Piper to incorporate a turboprop powerplant, in the form of two Pratt & Whitney Aircraft of Canada PT6As. With the introduction of a lower-cost PA-31T-1 Cheyenne I in 1978, the original PA-31T was renamed Cheyenne II and in October 1980 a PA-31T-2 Cheyenne IIXL was announced, with a fuselage 'stretched' by 2 ft 0 in (0.61 m) to provide more comfortable accommodation. All three versions remain available in 1983, as well as a Maritime Surveillance Cheyenne II.

Increasing demands for corporate and commuter airline transports led to introduction of the Cheyenne III in 1980. This differs from the Cheyenne I/II by having greater wing span, a T-tail, more powerful turboprops, and its fuselage lengthened by 8 ft 8¾ in (2.66 m) to seat a maximum of nine passengers. It is extensively equipped to standard, but a wide range of optional equipment and avionics is available including global navigation and autopilot/flight director systems. One Cheyenne III set 15 world speed records in the FAI Cle class during a round-the-world flight completed during 19-23 March 1982.

Specification: Piper PA-42 Cheyenne III
Origin: USA
Type: corporate and commuter transport
Accommodation: flight crew of 2; up to 9 passengers
Powerplant: two 720-shp (537-kW) Pratt & Whitney Aircraft of Canada PT6A-41 turboprops
Performance: maximum speed 341 mph (549 km/h); maximum cruising speed 334 mph (538 km/h) at 20,000 ft (6095 m); service ceiling 32,000 ft (9755 m); maximum range with fuel reserves 2,579 miles (4150 km)
Weights: empty 6,389 lb (2898 kg); maximum take-off 11,200 lb (5080 kg)
Dimensions: span 47 ft 8 in (14.53 m); length 43 ft 4¾ in (13.23 m); height 14 ft 9 in (4.50 m); wing area 293.0 sq ft (27.22 m²)

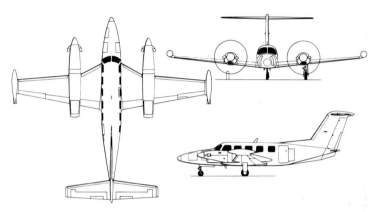

Piper PA-42 Cheyenne II

Piper Aircraft Corporation's Cheyenne I and II was complemented in 1980 by the entry into service of the Cheyenne III illustrated here. With maximum 11-seat capacity it has proved of interest to commuter airlines, its fuel-efficient turboprop powerplant giving it a sales advantage over piston-engined aircraft.

Saab-Fairchild Model 340 Commuter

Collaborative plans made by Saab-Scania in Sweden and Fairchild Industries in the United States came to fruition in early 1983 with the first flight, on schedule, of the Saab-Fairchild Model 340 Commuter. In addition to Airline and Commuter configurations, a 16-seat corporate/executive version is planned.

History and Notes

In recent years there have been several aircraft developed by international collaboration between manufacturers. The growing complexity and cost of new high-technology aircraft has placed even greater emphasis on the need for such associations, but that formed between Saab-Scania in Sweden and Fairchild Industries in the USA is, so far, unique. It is the first to unite European and US aerospace industries in the development of a civil transport aircraft.

Known as the Saab-Fairchild 340, this aircraft is designed for easy maintenance and quick turn-arounds without reliance upon airport ground-handling equipment. It has new-generation fuel-efficient wing-mounted turboprop engines and is configured as a cantilever low-wing monoplane with a circular-section pressurized fuselage, conventional tail unit and retractable tricycle landing gear with twin wheels on each unit. It is available in airline and corporate versions with standard seating for 34 and 16 passengers respectively.

The first prototype was rolled out on schedule at Linkoping, Sweden on 27 October 1982 and made its first flight on 25 January 1983; it will be used with the second prototype and first production aircraft to complete the certification programme. Firm orders and options then totalled more than 100 aircraft.

Specification: Saab-Fairchild 340 Commuter (airline)
Origin: International
Type: short-range transport
Accommodation: flight crew of 2 or 3; up to 34 passengers
Powerplant: two 1,630-shp (1215-kw) General Electric CT7-5A turboprops
Performance: (estimated) maximum cruising speed 315 mph (508 km/h) at 15,000 ft (4570 m); economic cruising speed 267 mph (430 km/h); service ceiling 25,000 ft (7620 m); range with 34 passengers and fuel reserves 1,048 miles (1687 km)
Weights: empty operating 15,860 lb (7194 kg); maximum take-off 26,000 lb (11793 kg)
Dimensions: span 70 ft 4 in (21.44 m); length 64 ft 6½ in (19.67 m); height 22 ft 6½ in (6.87 m); wing area 450.0 sq ft (41.81 m²)

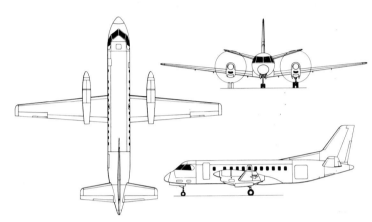

Saab-Fairchild 340

The Saab-Fairchild 340, which is expected to enter service in 1984, is pressurized and has an environmental control system as standard. Its full de-icing system includes pneumatic boots for wing and tailplane leading edges, with electrical anti-icing of windscreens, pitot heads, engine intakes and propellers.

Shorts SC.7 Skyvan/Skyliner

Skyvans have an easy-to-build fuselage of square cross-section, and one that provides maximum interior space. The side elevation of this profile emphasizes the positioning of the wing, clear of the cabin. This basic layout has been retained for the company's more recent products, the Shorts 330 and 360.

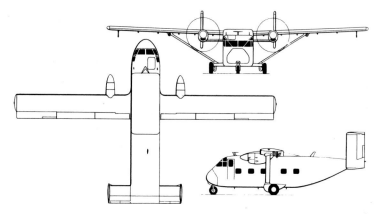

History and Notes

Derived from the Miles Aerovan that was developed just after World War II, the Shorts Series 1 Skyvan prototype (G-ASCN), intended as a low-cost utility aircraft, was first flown on 17 January 1963. A braced high-wing monoplane with a rectangular-section fuselage, a tail unit comprising twin fins and rudders, and with fixed tricycle landing gear, it included a full-width loading door in the undersurface of the upswept rear fuselage. As first flown it was powered by two 390-hp (291-kW) Continental GTSIO-520 piston engines. These were replaced later by the intended powerplant of 520-shp (388-kW) Turboméca Astazou II turboprops, the aircraft then becoming redesignated as the Series 1A.

The first production version, the Series 2, was powered by 730-eshp (544-ekW) Astazou XIIs, but a switch to Garrett TPE 331 turboprops in 1967 identified the Series 3 which is the current civil production version. It is available also in Series 3M and Series 3M-200 (higher gross weight) military versions, these being able to accommodate 22 fully-equipped troops, 16 paratroops and a dispatcher, or 12 stretcher cases and two medical attendants. A limited-production de luxe passenger version, with overhead baggage lockers, was developed as the Skyliner, but only nine of these were built. Orders for all versions total about 150.

Specification: Shorts Skyvan Series 3
Origin: UK
Type: civil utility transport
Accommodation: flight crew of 1 or 2; up to 19 passengers
Powerplant: two 715-shp (533-kW) Garrett TPE 331-201 turboprops
Performance: maximum cruising speed 203 mph (327 km/h) at 10,000 ft (3050 m); economic cruising speed 173 mph (278 km/h) at 10,000 ft (3050 m); service ceiling 22,500 ft (6860 m); maximum range with fuel reserves 694 miles (1117 km)
Weights: empty operating 8,100 lb (3674 kg); maximum take-off 12,500 lb (5670 kg)
Dimensions: span 64 ft 11 in (19.79 m); length 41 ft 4 in (12.60 m); height 15 ft 1 in (4.60 m); wing area 373.0 sq ft (34.65 m²)

Shorts SC.7 Skyvan Series 3

Despite having flown for the first time just over 20 years ago, the Shorts Skyvan remains in production in 1983 and is available in civil (Srs 3) and military (Srs 3M) versions. Illustrated is SX-BBO *Isle of Skiathos*, which is one of two Srs 3 Skyvans operated by Greece's government-owned Olympic Airways.

Shorts 330/Sherpa

Shorts Skyliner/Skyvan provided valuable experience in developing reliability, experience used in designing the 330. This kind of reliability was good enough for Command Airways of New York to acquire a fleet of six Shorts 330-100s which it uses to link points in New York with La Guardia and Kennedy airports.

History and Notes

It was once suggested that sales of the Short Skyvan might reach 1,000, but with only about nine aircraft per year built since 1966 it now seems unlikely that 25 per cent of this figure will be realized. The reason is that its market prospects are limited by capacity/performance: if either factor could be increased significantly then, theoretically, so would sales figures.

This thinking led Shorts to develop an aircraft similar to the Skyvan, but with seats for 30 passengers. The resulting Shorts 330 has many features of its predecessor, including its wide cabin, but one that is increased in length by 12 ft 5 in (3.78 m). The same overall configuration is retained, but retractable tricycle landing gear and improved lines help ensure that its two Pratt & Whitney PT6A turboprop engines can provide better performance. The first of two prototypes (G-BSBH) was flown on 22 August 1974 and initial deliveries made in June 1976. Three versions were available in 1983, the standard passenger 330-200, a Sherpa civil freighter which has a Skyvan-type rear loading door, and the 330-UTT military utility tactical transport. A total of 112 orders and options for all versions have been received, and of this number about 90 have been delivered. Major operators are Command Airways, Golden West Airlines, Metro Airlines, Mississippi Valley Airlines and Suburban Airlines.

Specification: Shorts 330-200
Origin: UK
Type: short-range transport
Accommodation: flight crew of 2; up to 30 passengers
Powerplant: two 1,198-shp (893-kW) Pratt & Whitney Aircraft of Canada PT6A-45R turboprops
Performance: maximum cruising speed 218 mph (351 km/h) at 10,000 ft (3050 m); economic cruising speed 184 mph (296 km/h) at 10,000 ft (3050 m); range with 30 passengers 553 miles (890 km)
Weights: empty equipped 14,700 lb (6668 kg); maximum take-off 22,900 lb (10387 kg)
Dimensions: span 74 ft 8 in (22.76 m); length 58 ft 0½ in (17.69 m); height 16 ft 3 in (4.95 m); wing area 453.0 sq ft (42.08 m²)

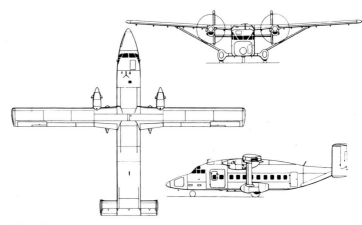

Shorts 330

Practicality rather than beauty of line dictated the shape of the Shorts 330, ensuring a wide unobstructed cabin. It can not only seat a worthwhile number of fare-paying passengers, but is equally at home with all-cargo or combinations of both. This flexibility appeals to commuter operators such as Golden West.

Shorts 360

In finalizing its configuration for the Shorts 360 (formerly SD3-60), the company clearly arrived at a capacity and performance capability which appealed to the US market. Almost half of the 112 ordered by early 1983 are in use with operators in North and South America.

History and Notes

Shorts announced on 10 July 1980 the introduction of a 'stretched' development of its Shorts 330, reflecting the buoyancy of the commuter airline market despite a general recession affecting so many airline operators. The type is designated Shorts 360, the numerical suffix indicating the 36-seat capacity of this new aircraft, which differs from its immediate predecessor in several respects. It retains the same basic configuration and, because it is intended for operation over short stage lengths and does not need cabin pressurization, has the same roomy cabin interior with dimensions of 6 ft 6 in (1.98 m) in height and width. It differs in having the fuselage lengthened by 3 ft 0 in (0.91 m), strengthened wing bracing struts and wing outer panels, and fuel-efficient engines of greater power. Most conspicuous of the changes is the adoption of a revised rear fuselage, incorporating a conventional tail unit with single fin and rudder. Intended to reduce drag, and hence increase fuel efficiency, this also provides greater baggage capacity.

The Shorts 360 prototype (G-ROOM), then powered by PT6A-45 turboprops, was flown on 1 June 1981. The intended PT6A-65R engines were installed subsequently and, following the first flight of a production aircraft on 19 August 1982, certification was gained on 3 September 1982. The first of four for Suburban Airlines of Reading, Pennsylvania entered service in November 1982, and Shorts have now received orders and options for some 30 of these aircraft.

Specification: Shorts 360

Origin: UK
Type: commuter transport
Accommodation: flight crew of 2; up to 36 passengers
Powerplant: two 1,327-shp (990-kW) Pratt & Whitney Aircraft of Canada PT6A-65R turboprops
Performance: cruising speed 243 mph (391 km/h); range with 36 passengers and fuel reserves 265 miles (426 km)
Weights: empty operating 16,600 lb (7530 kg); maximum take-off 25,700 lb (11657 kg)
Dimensions: span 74 ft 10 in (22.81 m); length 70 ft 10 in (21.59 m); height 23 ft 8 in (7.21 m); wing area 453.0 sq ft (42.08 m²)

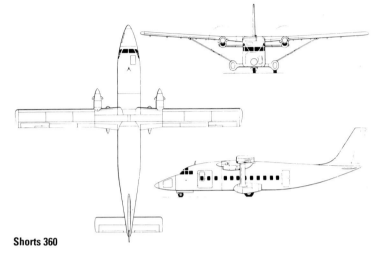

Shorts 360

The Shorts 360 illustrated, G-RMSS of Air Ecosse based at Aberdeen, Scotland, is one of five operated by this company in 1983. G-RMSS is used on the British Royal Mail's Datapost service, which provides fast and reliable overnight delivery for urgent packages within the UK and to some foreign destinations.

Sikorsky S-61

Okanagan Helicopters of British Columbia is numbered among the world's largest operators of helicopters. Its fleet includes a dozen S-61s, but only four are of the little-produced (total 13) non-amphibious S-61Ls. Perhaps this was seen as a limitation to the go-anywhere capability that is implied in a helicopter.

History and Notes

Developed to meet a US Navy requirement for a large-capacity ASW helicopter, Sikorsky's S-61 was built in military versions that included the S-61A amphibious transport, S-61B ASW aircraft and S-61R transports for the USAF/US Coast Guard. As the type proved reliable and safe, Sikorsky introduced civil transport versions, first being the S-61L, flown 6 December 1960. A non-amphibious version of the military S-61 with fixed tailwheel landing gear, the S-61L differed in its internal layout, accommodating a flight crew of two, a stewardess and up to 28 passengers. Certificated on 2 November 1961, the type entered revenue service with Los Angeles Airways on 1 March 1962. A fully-amphibious S-61N, flown on 7 August 1962, had its main landing gear units retracting into stabilizing floats. Both were certificated for all-weather operations and powered by General Electric CT-58-140 turboshaft engines. Late production S-61N-IIs have more powerful CT58-140-1/2 turboshafts and seat up to 30 passengers.

Production of S-61Ls and S-61Ns by Sikorsky ended in June 1980 after construction of 13 and 123 respectively, but Agusta in Italy has acquired production rights and planned to produce a modified AS-61N1 in 1983. Major operators include Bristow Helicopters, British Airways Helicopters, Greenlandair, Helikopter Service A/S, and Okanagan Helicopters.

Specification: Sikorsky S-61N
Origin: USA
Type: transport helicopter
Accommodation: flight crew of 2; up to 30 passengers
Powerplant: two 1,500-shp (1119-kW) General Electric CT58-140-1/2 turboshafts
Performance: maximum cruising speed 150 mph (241 km/h); economic cruising speed 138 mph (222 km/h); service ceiling 12,500 ft (3810 m); range with maximum fuel and reserves 495 miles (797 km)
Weights: empty 12,510 lb (5674 kg); maximum take-off 20,500 lb (9299 kg)
Dimensions: main rotor diameter 62 ft 0 in (18.90 m); length, rotors turning 72 ft 10 in (22.20 m); height 17 ft 5½ in (5.32 m); main rotor disc area 3,019.0 sq ft (280.47 m²)

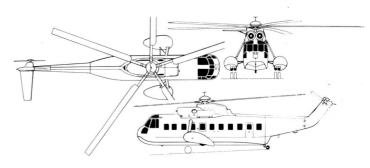

Sikorsky S-61N

Following the development of an amphibious military transport for the US Navy (SH-3 Sea King), Sikorsky evolved civil versions of this large design which had the model identification S-61. Most extensively built was the S-61N shown here, which had a sealed hull and stabilizing floats to give amphibious capability.

Sikorsky S-76 Spirit

This Sikorsky S-76 of Petroleum Helicopters is an example of an early model but S-76 Mk IIs, which entered production in early 1982, included more than 40 improvements. Available in 1983 are Utility, and EMS (emergency medical service) versions, and an S-76 Military with a variety of weapons is under development.

History and Notes

Growing demands for transport helicopters in support of offshore energy operations led Sikorsky to initiate worldwide market research to establish the requirements of such operators. An important factor to which the company needed an answer was seating capacity, and in 1975 was able to begin the development of a 14-seat commercial helicopter designated S-76 and later named Spirit. The first of four prototypes (N762SA) was flown on 13 March 1977, and the first fully certificated IFR production aircraft was delivered to Air Logistics of Lafayette, Louisiana on 27 February 1979.

This short certification programme resulted from the use of an advanced dynamic system/powerplant combination evolved for military requirements, but further development continued from the time that production began, leading to an improved S-76 Mark II from 1 March 1982. This differs by having improved cabin ventilation, dynamic system refinements, more access panels to simplify maintenance, and an advanced version of the Allison 250 turboshaft which gives an increase in guaranteed power output. In May 1982 Sikorsky announced three other versions: a more basic S-76 Utility, S-76 Military and an S-76EMS for emergency medical service. Sales now total about 400, of which almost half have been delivered.

Specification: Sikorsky S-76 Mark II
Origin: USA
Type: utility transport helicopter
Accommodation: flight crew of 2; up to 12 passengers
Powerplant: two 682-shp (509-kW) Allison 250-C30S turboshafts
Performance: maximum cruising speed 167 mph (269 km/h); economic cruising speed 144 mph (232 km/h); service ceiling 15,000 ft (4570 m); range with 12 passengers and fuel reserves 465 miles (748 km)
Weights: empty equipped 5,600 lb (2540 kg); maximum take-off 10,300 lb (4672 kg)
Dimensions: main rotor diameter 44 ft 0 in (13.41 m); length, rotors turning 52 ft 6 in (16.00 m); height 14 ft 5¾ in (4.41 m); main rotor disc area 1,257.0 sq ft (116.78 m²)

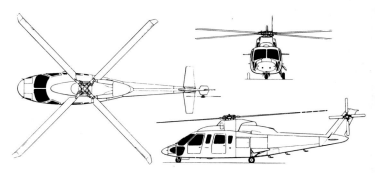

Sikorsky S-76 Spirit

In a different class of helicopter to its S-61, Sikorsky's S-76 Spirit is proving of interest to operators providing communication with offshore resources. Air Logistics, a major US rotary-wing operator, has more than a dozen S-76 Spirits in its large and varied fleet of predominantly Bell helicopters.

The Brazilian third-level airline Votec Servicos Aereos Regionais operates a large and mixed fleet of both fixed- and rotary-wing aircraft, almost 75 per cent of the total being helicopters. In addition to operating scheduled passenger services, the helicopters are available on an air taxi or charter basis.

(Fairchild) Swearingen Metro/Metro II/III

For airlines like Colombia's Tavina (Transportes Colombiana de Aviacion SA), with a mix of charter, scheduled passenger and cargo operations, the Metro provides essential flexibility. Passenger and/or cargo doors give multi-role access, and stowing/folding seats and movable bulkheads simplify loading problems.

History and Notes

Swearingen Aviation Corporation, known since January 1981 as Fairchild Swearingen Corporation, began the design of a 20-seat commuter transport in the late 1960s. The resulting SA226-TC Metro was flown for the first time on 26 August 1969, being certificated in June 1970, but did not enter service until 1973, initially with Commuter Airlines of Binghampton, New York. A fairly conventional low-wing monoplane, it had a circular-section pressurized fuselage, a tail unit with all-swept surfaces, retractable tricycle landing gear and two wing-mounted Garrett TPE331 turboprop engines.

The Metro was followed by an improved Metro II, incorporating larger cabin windows and detail refinements, but the current production version in 1982 is the SA227-AC Metro III. This introduces many improvements, the most important being a 10 ft 0 in (3.05 m) increase in wing span, more powerful engines, new main landing gear doors and system refinements. A Metro IIIA is also available, differing by having Pratt & Whitney Aircraft of Canada PT6A-45R turboprops in place of Garrett engines, plus a number of other improvements. An 8/11-seat executive transport version of the Metro III is available as the Merlin IIIC and a 13/16-seat corporate transport as the Merlin IVC. A total of 236 Metros of all versions had been sold by mid-1982, these being in service with 44 airlines worldwide.

Specification: Fairchild Swearingen Metro III
Origin: USA
Type: commuter transport
Accommodation: flight crew of 2; up to 20 passengers
Powerplant: two 1,100-shp (820-kW) Garrett TPE 331-11U-601G turboprops
Performance: maximum cruising speed 320 mph (515 km/h) at 15,000 ft (4570 m); service ceiling 27,500 ft (8380 m); range with 19 passengers and fuel reserves 1,000 miles (1610 km)
Weights: empty operating 8,737 lb (3963 kg); maximum take-off 14,500 lb (6577 kg)
Dimensions: span 57 ft 0 in (17.37 m); length 59 ft 4¼ in (18.09 m); height 16 ft 8 in (5.08 m); wing area 309.0 sq ft (28.71 m²)

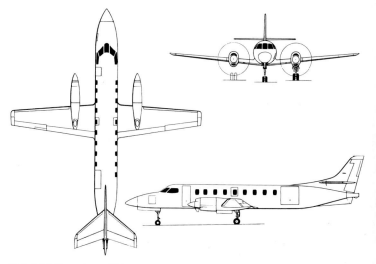

(Fairchild) Swearingen Metro

Changing fortunes in the North American aerospace industry resulted in Edward Swearingen's company becoming a subsidiary of Fairchild Industries in 1979. This meant that Metros acquired the name prefix Fairchild Swearingen. In 1983 the founding name has gone, but Fairchild Aircraft Metros continue in production.

Crossair AG, based at Zurich, Switzerland, is a comparatively new but busy operator, known originally as Business-Flyers Basel when formed in 1975. This Metro II is one of a fleet of IIs and IIIs which the company uses to operate a network of scheduled passengers services linking Zurich with European cities.

Tupolev Tu-124 'Cookpot'

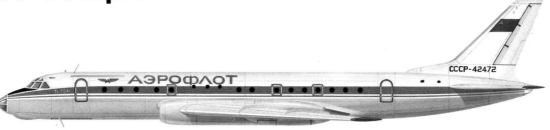

When the Tupolev Tu-124 entered service on Aeroflot's Moscow-Tallin route on 2 October 1962, it was the first turbofan-powered commercial transport to be used on regular air services anywhere in the world. By comparison with the turbojet, the turbofan engine has better specific fuel consumption and is less noisy.

History and Notes

Although there was no doubt that the Tu-104 had brought a dramatic change in flight times over routes operated by it, there was criticism of the high operating costs resulting from its comparatively undeveloped turbojet engines. This criticism was tempered, however, by the fact that Aeroflot desperately needed aircraft of such capability. A requirement for a short/medium-range airliner to replace piston-engined Ilyushin Il-14s in service, and combining an ability to operate from unprepared or short airstrips with more efficient engines, presented something of a challenge for the Tupolev design bureau.

It was decided to develop a reduced-scale version of the Tu-104, incorporating aerodynamic and systems refinements to give the necessary short-field performance, and newly-developed and much more efficient turbofan engines to power what was designated the Tu-124. The Soloviev D-20P two-spool turbofans installed in these aircraft were, in fact, the first engines of this type to equip any of the world's short/medium-range airliners. Tu-124s with seats for 44 passengers entered service with Aeroflot on 10 November 1962, but the standard Tu-124V had 56 seats. Other versions included the Tu-124K and Tu-124K2 with de luxe seating for 36 and 22 passengers respectively. About 100 were built, but Aeroflot has now retired its Tu-124s from service.

Specification: Tupolev Tu-124V
Origin: USSR
Type: short/medium-range transport
Accommodation: flight crew of 3; up to 56 passengers
Powerplant: two 11,905-lb (5400-kg) thrust Soloviev D-20P turbofans
Performance: maximum speed 603 mph (970 km/h) at 26,245 ft (8000 m); economic cruising speed 497 mph (800 km/h); service ceiling 38,385 ft (11700 m); range with maximum payload 758 miles (1220 km)
Weights: empty 49,604 lb (22500 kg); maximum take-off 83,776 lb (38000 kg)
Dimensions: span 83 ft 9¾ in (25.55 m); length 100 ft 4 in (30.58 m); height 26 ft 6 in (8.08 m); wing area 1,280.95 sq ft (119.00 m²)

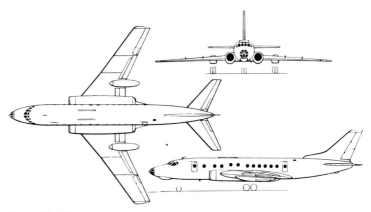

Tupolev Tu-124

In addition to their use by Aeroflot, Tupolev Tu-124s were operated by CSA in Czechoslovakia and by Interflug in East Germany. A number also entered military service, and it is believed that small numbers still remain in use in a VIP transport role with the air forces of East Germany, India and Iraq.

Tupolev Tu-134 'Crusty'

Representing initially a continuing development of the Tu-104/-124 family, and in fact designated originally Tu-124A, Tupolev's Tu-134 ended by being sufficiently different to warrant a new and separate designation. The main changes were its rear-mounted powerplant and the incorporation of a T-tail.

History and Notes

Tupolev's bureau was probably elated by the success of Tu-104s and Tu-124s in use by Aeroflot, but must have been concerned that neither had attracted any export orders. This resulted in a version of the Tu-124 with a more interesting interior layout. Allocated the provisional designation Tu-124A, the aircraft retained wings, fuselage and landing gear that were generally similar, but in two aspects this aircraft was completely different. Firstly, the turbofan powerplant was removed from the wings, ensuring 'clean' aerodynamic surfaces unaffected by engine intake/efflux and the airflow around nacelles, and mounted instead on the rear fuselage. Secondly, this resulted in replacement of the conventional tail unit by a T-tail, and because of these changes the Tu-124A was redesignated Tu-134.

The first Tu-134, powered by two Soloviev D-30 turbofans and seating up to 72 passengers, entered service with Aeroflot in September 1967, but the Tu-134A, introduced in 1970, had a fuselage lengthened by 6 ft 10½ in (2.10 m) to seat up to 84. With this aircraft Tupolev achieved some export success and it has been built in larger numbers. The most recent version, which probably began to enter service during 1982, is the Tu-134B with seats for up to 90 passengers. Production is estimated as 650-700, the majority in current service, with Aeroflot and Interflug as major operators.

Specification: Tupolev Tu-134A
Origin: USSR
Type: short/medium-range transport
Accommodation: flight crew of 3; up to 84 passengers
Powerplant: two 14,991-lb (6800-kg) thrust Soloviev D-30 Srs II turbofans
Performance: maximum cruising speed 550 mph (885 km/h); economic cruising speed 466 mph (750 km/h); service ceiling 39,010 ft (11890 m); range with maximum payload 1,174 miles (1890 km)
Weights: empty operating 64,044 lb (29050 kg); maximum take-off 103,617 lb (47000 kg)
Dimensions: span 95 ft 1¾ in (29.00 m); length 121 ft 6¾ in (37.05 m); height 30 ft 0 in (9.15 m); wing area 1,370.29 sq ft (127.30 m²)

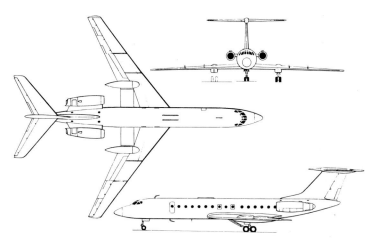

Tupolev Tu-134A

Production and development of the Tupolev Tu-134 is continuing, and more than 600 are believed to be in current airline service. Illustrated is the Tu-134A YU-AHX *Beograd* of Yugoslavia's Aviogenex, but the largest non-Aeroflot fleet is operated by Interflug, the national airline of the German Democratic Republic.

Tupolev Tu-154 'Careless'

Aeroflot operates about 475 of the 520 Tupolev Tu-154s in service in early 1983. The remainder are shared between Alyemda, Balkan Bulgarian, Choson Minhang, Cubana, Malev and Tarom. Illustrated is Tu-154B-2 HA-LCM, one of 10 operated by the Hungarian State airline Malev on European and Near East routes.

History and Notes

In the mid-1960s Tupolev's bureau received a challenging requirement, the design of an aircraft to replace Antonov An-10s, Ilyushin Il-18s and Tupolev Tu-104s in service. Such an airliner needed to combine the secondary field performance of the An-10, range capability of the Il-18 and speed of the Tu-104. The resulting Tu-154 resembles but is slightly larger than the Boeing 727, and shares the same rear-mounted three-engined layout. It is a low-wing monoplane with a circular-section pressurized fuselage, T-tail and retractable tricycle landing gear which has a six-wheel bogie on each main unit. The initial Tu-154s evaluated in 1971 were powered by 20,944-lb (9500-kg) thrust Kuznetsov NK-8-2 turbofans.

Aeroflot's first Tu-154 services began on 8 February 1972. Since then the improved Tu-154A and Tu-154B have been developed, both with more powerful engines, greater fuel capacity and performance/reliability refinements. The Tu-154B differs by having a slightly longer cabin, without change in fuselage dimensions, to accommodate up to 169 passengers. Tu-154As and Tu-154Bs are believed to have entered service in 1975 and 1978 respectively. Since then a Tu-154B-2, incorporating refinements, and a mixed passenger/cargo Tu-154M have been reported. Production of all versions is believed to be over 500, the majority still remaining in service, with Aeroflot, Balkan Bulgarian Airlines and Tarom the major operators.

Specification: Tupolev Tu-154A
Origin: USSR
Type: medium/long-range transport
Accommodation: flight crew of 3 or 4; up to 168 passengers
Powerplant: three 23,149-lb (10500-kg) thrust Kuznetsov NK-8-2U turbofans
Performance: cruising speed 559 mph (900 km/h) at 39,370 ft (12000 m); range with maximum payload and fuel reserves 1,709 miles (2750 km)
Weights: empty operating 111,940 lb (50775 kg); maximum take-off 207,235 lb (94000 kg)
Dimensions: span 123 ft 2¼ in (37.55 m); length 157 ft 1¾ in (47.90 m); height 37 ft 4¾ in (11.40 m); wing area 2,168.46 sq ft (201.45 m²)

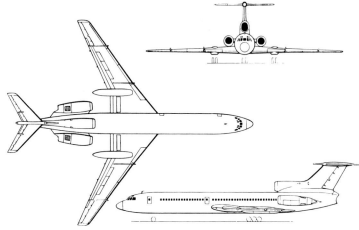

Tupolev Tu-154

Cubana numbers three Tupolev Tu-154s among its almost all-Soviet fleet of aircraft. Illustrated is CU-T1222, a Tu-154B-2, which finds employment on the airline's international routes. This version has a number of refinements and incorporates Thomson-CSF/SFIM automatic flight control and navigation systems.

Vickers Viscount

Numbers of around 100 Viscounts in service in 1982 had dwindled to about 60 in early 1983. British Midland and British Air Ferries have about a third of this number, but it is inevitable that soon the Viscount will live on only in history, the first turbine-powered transport in scheduled passenger service.

History and Notes

Named originally Viceroy, but renamed Viscount after India became an independent state within the British Commonwealth, the Vickers Type 630 prototype was first flown on 16 July 1948. Then powered by four 1,380-eshp (1029-ekW) Rolls-Royce RDa.I Mk 502 turboprop engines, providing impressive and smooth performance, the Type 630 failed to attract any interest because of its 32-seat capacity. Fortunately, a more powerful version of the Dart became available, leading to a Type 700 Viscount which was acceptable to British European Airways (BEA) and could seat up to 43 passengers. The first production Viscount for BEA was flown on 20 August 1952, certificated on 17 April 1953, and was used to inaugurate Viscount services between London and Cyprus on the following day.

A mass of orders for this attractive transport followed, including significant numbers for North America, and it seemed that at last the British industry had broken into the American market. Such hopes were premature, but the Viscount retains the record of being the UK's most extensively built airliner, production totalling 444. These included the Type 700D seating up to 59, the lengthened fuselage (by 3 ft 10 in/1.17 m) Type 800 seating up to 71, and the Type 810 for operation at higher gross weight. Only about 60 of these aircraft now remain in service, used by more than 30 airlines, with British Midland Airways the major operator.

Specification: Vickers Type 810 Viscount
Origin: UK
Type: short/medium-range transport
Accommodation: flight crew of 2 or 3; up to 71 passengers
Powerplant: four 2,100-eshp (1566-ekW) Rolls-Royce Dart RDa.7/1 Mk 525 turboprops
Performance: maximum cruising speed 350 mph (563 km/h) at 20,000 ft (6095 m); service ceiling 25,000 ft (7620 m); range with maximum payload 1,725 miles (2776 km)
Weights: empty operating 41,565 lb (18854 kg); maximum take-off 72,500 lb (32885 kg)
Dimensions: span 93 ft 8½ in (28.56 m); length 85 ft 8 in (26.11 m); height 26 ft 9 in (8.15 m); wing area 963.0 sq ft (89.46 m^2)

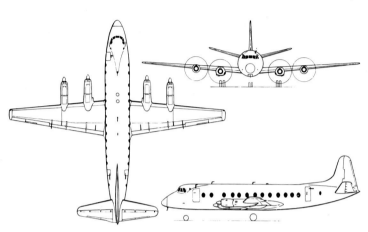

Vickers Type 800 Viscount

The Vickers Viscount, now beginning to be replaced in service by aircraft of a newer generation, was one of the designs that stemmed from the World War II Brabazon Committee's recommendations. Its aim was to get Britain's aircraft industry back into the civil aircraft market and the Viscount came nearest to success.

Westland 30

Airspur Inc, a new airline established at Los Angeles, California, received the first three of six Westland 30s on order (plus 15 options) in late 1982. They have been used to inaugurate a commuter service between Los Angeles International Airport and Fullerton, their 19-seat capacity ideal for this purpose.

History and Notes

In 1976 Westland Helicopters began development of a large-fuselage variant of the Lynx military helicopter under the designation Westland 30, and the first of two prototypes (G-BGHF) was flown initially on 10 April 1979. Of conventional helicopter configuration, the Westland 30 has four-blade main and tail rotors, a horizontal stabilizer with endplate fins, non-retractable tricycle landing gear as standard (retractable optional) and power provided by two Rolls-Royce Gem turboshafts. Standard accommodation of the civil version is for a crew of one or two plus 17 passengers, but high-density seating allows for 19 passengers. The Series 100 production version entered service with British Airways Helicopters on 6 January 1983, a second example being delivered during October 1982. VFR and IFR certification was gained in the UK and the USA during March and December 1982 respectively. Other deliveries have included three to Airspur Inc. of Los Angeles in late 1982, with three for Airspur (Series 100-60 with 1,180-shp/880-kW Gem 60-3 engines) and two for Helicopter Hire of Southend, Essex planned during 1982. Civil versions can be equipped for passenger/cargo transport, offshore rig support and executive/VIP use; military versions are planned for aeromedical, battlefield support and tactical transport roles.

Specification: Westland 30 Series 100
Origin: UK
Type: general-purpose helicopter
Accommodation: flight crew of 1/2 and a maximum of 19 passengers
Powerplant: two 1,000-shp (746-kW) Rolls-Royce Gem 41-1 turboshafts
Performance: maximum cruising speed 138 mph (222 km/h) at sea level; range with 4,000-lb (1814-kg) internal payload and no reserves 219 miles (352 km)
Weights: empty 6,982 lb (3167 kg); maximum take-off weight 12,350 lb (5602 kg)
Dimensions: main rotor diameter 43 ft 8 in (13.31 m); length, rotors turning 52 ft 2 in (15.90 m); height 15 ft 6 in (4.72 m); main rotor disc area 1,497.70 sq ft (139.14 m²)

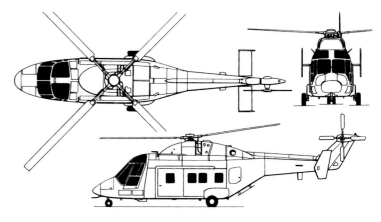

Westland 30

This is the prototype Westland 30, seen in the colours of Airspur. The British government has provided Westland with funding to speed development of improved versions, which are designated Westland 30-200 and -300.

Yakovlev Yak-40 'Codling'

After Aeroflot, Balkan Bulgarian Airlines is the most important user of the Yak-40, with a fleet of 15 in 1983. The Yak-40 is, curiously, yet another Douglas DC-3 replacement, developed to supersede the Lisunov Li-2, an extensively built version of the Douglas DC-3 first used during World War II.

History and Notes

Designed in the early 1960s as a feederliner to replace Lisunov Li-2s (Soviet-built DC-3s) in Aeroflot service, the Yak-40 feederliner was destined to be built in large numbers if it met Aeroflot's requirements successfully. To fulfil the role it needed to operate effectively from grass airfields or semi-prepared strips, dictating a design which incorporated high-lift lightly-loaded wings, plus the added safety of three- rather than two-engined powerplant. A cantilever low-wing monoplane with a circular-section fuselage, T-tail, retractable tricycle landing gear and rear-mounted Ivchenko AI-25 turbofans, the first prototype made its maiden flight on 21 October 1966.

Production aircraft were first used for revenue services by Aeroflot on 30 September 1968 and when production ended, during 1979-80, it was believed that close on 1,000 had been built for Aeroflot and for export. Accommodation on the flight deck allows for a crew of two or three, and a variety of cabin arrangements caters for a maximum of 32 passengers. For operation from airfields with minimum facilities, the Yak-40 has a ventral door with airstair at the rear of the cabin, and an auxiliary power unit mounted in the fin fairing makes the aircraft independent of ground facilities for starting and the maintenance of air-conditioning/heating. Well over 700 Yak-40s still remain in serivice, the major operators being Aeroflot, Balkan Bulgarian Airlines and CSA Czechoslovak Airlines.

Specification: Yakovlev Yak-40
Origin: USSR
Type: short-range transport
Accommodation: flight crew of 2 or 3; up to 32 passengers
Powerplant: three 3,307-lb (1500-kg) thrust Ivchenko AI-25 turbofans
Performance: maximum cruising speed 342 mph (550 km/h) at 23,000 ft (7010 m); range with 32 passengers and fuel reserves 901 miles (1450 km)
Weights: empty 20,723 lb (9400 kg); maximum take-off 35,274 lb (16000 kg)
Dimensions: span 82 ft 0¼ in (25.00 m); length 66 ft 9½ in (20.36 m); height 21 ft 3¾ in (6.50 m); wing area 753.5 sq ft (70.00 m²)

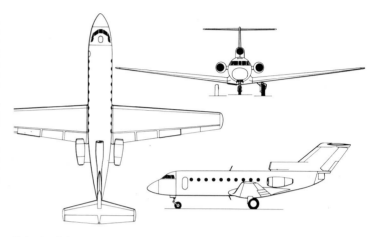

Yakovlev Yak-40

About 800 Yakovlev Yak-40 short-range transports were in airline service in early 1983, more than 90 per cent of them operated by Aeroflot. This view of the Yak-40 emphasizes the neat installation of its three rear-mounted turbofan engines and the upswept rear fuselage which incorporates a ventral airstair.

Yakovlev Yak-42 'Clobber'

Yakovlev Yak-42 CCCP-42304 shown in the accompanying picture and CCCP-42304, the subject of this profile, are now in service with Aeroflot. About 40 were thought to have been delivered by early 1983. It can take off safely after a failure of any one engine and can maintain flight on the power of a single engine.

History and Notes

With the requirement for a medium-range transport to replace Ilyushin Il-18s and Tupolev Tu-134s then in Aeroflot service, Yakovlev decided to benefit from its considerable experience with the Yak-40. From it the company has developed a larger-capacity version of generally similar configuration under the designation Yak-42. The first of three prototypes, with 11° wing sweep, was flown on 7 March 1975; the second and third prototypes had 23° wing sweep and, following flight evaluation, the latter configuration was chosen for production aircraft. The Yak-42 also differs from the Yak-40 by having all-swept surfaces for the T-tail, twin wheels on each landing gear unit and, of course, more powerful turbofan engines.

The first production aircraft began to enter scheduled service with Aeroflot in late 1980s, these having a single passenger cabin with seats for a maximum of 120 passengers. An alternative 100-passenger local-service layout is available, this having forward and rear carry-on baggage and coat storage compartments, and it is expected that a 'stretched' 140-passenger version will be certificated during 1983. There are provisions for a convertible passenger/cargo interior and the whole accommodation is pressurized and air-conditioned. It is believed that about 40 are now in service with Aeroflot and that initial deliveries of seven ordered by Aviogenex in Yugoslavia may have been made.

Specification: Yakovlev Yak-42
Origin: USSR
Type: medium-range transport
Accommodation: flight crew of 2; up to 120 passengers
Powerplant: three 14,330-lb (6500-kg) thrust Lotarev D-36 turbofans
Performance: maximum cruising speed 503 mph (810 km/h) at 25,000 ft (7620 m); economic cruising speed 466 mph (750 km/h); range with maximum payload 559 miles (900 km)
Weights: empty 63,845 lb (28960 kg); maximum take-off 117,947 lb (53.500 kg)
Dimensions: span 112 ft 2½ in (34.20 m); length 119 ft 4¼ in (36.38 m); height 32 ft 1¾ in (9.80 m); wing area 1,614.64 sq ft (150.00 m²)

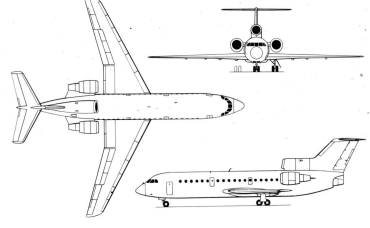

Yakovlev Yak-42

The Yakovlev Yak-42 CCCP-42303 illustrated is the third prototype of this medium-range turbofan-powered transport. It was developed to provide feederline services for Aeroflot's main trans-Siberian trunk routes, and special efforts were made to produce a reliable and economical design of simple construction.

Index